WINNING YEAR ONE

Jump-Start Student Success From Day 1

Carol Fuery

Ninth Edition
Revised
Sanibel SandDollar, Captiva, Florida

Dedication

My two favorite teachers are my parents, Polly and Jim Bailey. They brought up four children. They had lots of love to share and plenty of time to listen. Every night we had dinners at six p.m. sharp. And we enjoyed lively discussions, laughter and tears. They were good teachers who opened that first door for me, encouraged me and had the courage to discipline. They taught me all I know. They gave themselves to me so that I could give myself to you.

Winning Year One
Jump-Start Student Success From Day 1

Published by: Sanibel SandDollar Publishing
P.O. Box 461, Captiva FL 33924
239-472-3459 telephone   239-472-0699 fax

Ninth Printing 2005
Copyright 1986, 1987, 1988, 1989, 1991,1993,1997, 2000, 2005

by Carol Fuery

Cover design: Ruth Kuttler, Advanced Internet & Design Concepts, Naples, Florida

Typography: The Set Up, Inc., Cape Coral, Florida

ISBN 0-944295-07-X

Printed in the United States of America

www.carolfuery.com

Preface

The first year isn't easy. You're making the transition from student to educator almost overnight, but you're ready for the challenges. You'll meet experienced, talented teachers. Adopt one who's cheerful.

Good teaching looks perfectly natural, but it's not. Teachers aren't born; they're created. Expert teaching is learned behavior that takes years.

The colleagues and students who trained me were patient. Be patient with yourself and give teaching at least a two-year internship. By year three, you just may decide that teaching fits your personality.

My advice to you is to experiment, take risks and learn to love some of your most unlovable students.

Whether you're a new teacher just beginning your profession or a veteran recognizing yourself in these pages, *Winning Year One* will give you some ammunition to carry into the classroom.

There is no test at the end and nothing to memorize -- just quick reading and practical encouragement to make this **your winning year**. Enjoy!

Carol Fuery

Contents

Contents

About the Author

Carol Fuery is the author of more than 6 books. A teacher for 35 years, her book, *Winning Year One*, has sold over 107,000 copies — a best-seller!

Her other popular titles include: *Still Teaching After All These Years, Successful Substitute Teaching* and *Discipline Strategies for the Bored, Ballistic and Belligerent in Your Classroom.*

A native Floridian, Carol graduated from Florida Atlantic University and holds a Master's degree from Nova University.

An avid golfer, she lives with her husband, George Ruot, on Sanibel Island, Florida. Their daughter, Lisa Hendrix, is an elementary teacher and mother of two little angels, Ashley and Benjamin.

Carol Fuery's greatest wish is that one day her angels will become teachers.

1 Discipline With Dignity
Saving Face

In the beginning of my teaching career, I was the expert. Straight from college, I was cool, cocky and self-confident. I was also completely oblivious to my ignorance. I believed that my enthusiasm would excite my young charges to want to learn.

I'd be a smash in the classroom. Did I worry about discipline? Of course not.

I was as unconcerned as Alfred E. Neuman, listening impatiently and a little bored at the opening faculty meeting. Then the principal said something I'll never forget.

He said, "Every discipline problem in the classroom is caused by the teacher." I didn't believe it. Now, years later, I understand what that wise man meant.

Do teachers cause their own discipline problems? Yes, we do, by unconsciously encouraging bad behavior. It helps to remember that all behavior, both our students and our own, is purposeful.

All Behavior Is Purposeful

The reason may be unclear to us why our student, Sally, acts disrespectfully, but you can bet there's a reason behind her actions.

Sometimes teachers make bad behavior rewarding. One way to create a multitude of discipline problems is to set

1

yourself up as a dictator. Remember me, the expert? Well I did just that.

Tough Strategy

I began teaching in a junior high school. I was assigned a low-ability, unruly class of seventh graders. I anticipated trouble, and I got plenty. My strategy was to be tough. Too tough.

After that first week of school, my young charges greeted me with the Nazi stance and a "Heil, Hitler!" That gives you some indication of my personality. I was so afraid that my students would "take advantage of me" that I became unreasonable. It wasn't long before I hated the school, the kids, and in reality, myself. The discipline problems I created could have been avoided.

First, I needed to learn that it was possible to be myself and maintain discipline. However, because I was guided by fear, it was difficult for me to be a sincere, caring adult. I made the mistake of setting myself up as Head Honcho, King of the Mountain, daring my students to knock me from my throne of power.

Our students know how to wield power. They can be wonderful at defeating adults. They've had years of practice at home and in school.

King of the Mountain

Ever played King of the Mountain? It's a simple game that requires only a small hill. One child climbs to the top of the hill, and he/she is declared King until knocked down. Only one individual can be King at a time, and naturally, my three brothers and I were ruthless. Being at the top was a short-lived pleasure but worth all the pain. What glory to stand even momentarily with hands braced on hips and survey the world!

Classroom Dictator

Playing dictator within the classroom is a lot like playing King of the Mountain, it's a heady experience. But try to be King for a Year, and you ignite a series of discipline problems. I made this mistake the first week of school and soon realized that I was outnumbered. Students love to see dictators dethroned. As a new teacher, you've had little practice running a successful kingdom.

The Power of Anger

Another trick I learned early in this teaching business was the power of anger. I spent a lot of emotional energy getting mad in my Hitler days. My anger covered much territory. Sometimes it worked well. But many times it was a short-term gain for a long-term loss.

An angry teacher loses self-control. When angry, I can be most destructive with phrases that attack the student. These phrases include some all-time winners like, "You're such a jerk." "How could you do something so stupid?" These statements attack a student's character without solving the problem.

Maintain Composure

I needed to maintain my composure so that I could send out better messages. Statements like, "I'm annoyed," or "I'm furious," get the idea across without insult.

When I decided to use anger, I was silently telling my students, "Pay attention to me. I don't like what you're doing." Anger gave me a reward; it made me feel better.

For instance, say I assign an essay, but my students decide to talk instead of work. I yell, "Get quiet," or that old standby, "Shut up!" Silence. Want to place bets on how long it lasts? Not long. But I have my reward -- a few minutes of peace. The best part is that I'm not tense any more.

Teachers Do Get Angry

Good, experienced teachers *do* get angry. We aren't martyrs or masochists. It is okay to be frustrated, annoyed and aggravated. But we need to express the anger without the insult. Attack the behavior, not the child.

Good Discipline Means Saving Face

So, the key to good discipline is teacher self-control. Good discipline involves saving face for both the teacher and the student. While it may feel satisfying and help temporarily, anger doesn't wear well over the years.

I use a discipline maneuver that works. It saves the student's pride. Teachers can deflect a small problem before it gets a chance to ignite. When I give workshops for teachers, I demonstrate this technique. Most people are surprised at its simplicity. I call it my $1000 tip. Why? It has saved me $1000 worth of classroom hassles and Excedrin headaches.

4

The $1000 Discipline Tip

Let's set the scene. You have given the assignment. You walk around the room. This keeps the students on task. You're in control of the situation, answering questions and making sure everyone is working.

On your beat, you notice talkative George. He's turned around at his desk and is trying to get a conversation started with Joe. You cannot ignore this minor problem.

Step 1:

As a first approach, stare at George. Your scowl may be enough incentive to get George working . If his challenge continues and he ignores you, then try...

Step 2:

Walk over to him. Place your hand on his desk or on his elbow. The idea is to be physically close. You can't successfully discipline students unless you have their attention and you are physically close. This rule applies to the first grader as well as the high school senior.

Step 3:

Use the student's name. Give this simple command in a soft whisper. Remember that George is the only person who needs to hear the request. Say "George, do your vocabulary." Or "George, complete your math." Remember to use the student's name and to keep your command as direct and simple as possible. This lets George know exactly what he needs to do. You haven't embarrassed him or insulted his integrity.

Step 4:

Say nothing. To ensure that you say nothing, start counting silently. How long? Sixty seconds or less. You're waiting for George to respond to your command. You are not begging or pleading. You're in control of your behavior. Continue to stand near George. Your physical presence alone is a big factor in getting him back on task. At this point, George is now working.

Step 5:

Say, "Thank you, George." Always say, "Thank you," and always use the student's name. You haven't responded with anger. You have rewarded the good behavior by thanking him. This small discipline technique gets the student back on task. But more importantly, it also establishes a positive feeling between you and the young person.

The above technique is wonderfully effective. I've seen it work with six foot seniors as well as third graders. Why? I think part of the answer is that the teacher has changed his or her behavior. The only behavior I can really honestly control is my own. I can't possibly predict every reaction I may receive from a student, but I can control my own responses. That's the secret of good classroom discipline.

But what if I decide to ignore George? His behavior really isn't so bad, is it? If I ignore George, it won't take long for the entire class to be in an uproar of chatter. Young people are great observers. If we ignore one student who doesn't work very soon, we'll have a classroom that doesn't work. The student reasons, "If I can get away with misbehavior, then this teacher doesn't care about me."

If we care, then we have the courage to guide young people into doing what we know is right. Basically, students want to please the adults around them. Be the leader they crave. Guide them into responsible behavior.

Summary:

1. *Good discipline means teacher self-control.*
2. *Anger doesn't pay.*
3. *Gain the rewards.*
4. *Use the $1000 Discipline Plan:*
   - *Stare.*
   - *Get close.*
   - *Use the student's name.*
   - *Give a command.*
   - *Say nothing.*
   - *Thank the student using his/her name.*

2 Managing Feelings and Correcting Behavior

Perhaps there's a student who constantly resists your guidance. This young person is determined to misbehave. Then it's necessary to look at some of the feelings that provoke this unacceptable behavior.

Sue's Feelings

I recall Sue, an exceptionally intelligent girl in my tenth-grade class. She qualified for the gifted program, but at that time, our school didn't have one. On her good days, she simply acted superior to others. On her bad days, she attacked both my authority and her classmates.

During one class session, Sue was daydreaming. She sat slumped at her desk, obviously bored with the lesson. When I had the students break into groups, she refused to sit near anyone else or cooperate. I told Sue that I'd see her during the last five minutes of class.

My Conference Area

I have an area set up at the back of my classroom. It contains two comfortable chairs, my desk and a filing cabinet. The area offers some privacy, and at the same time, I can still observe the classroom.

I had Sue sit in one of the comfortable chairs near my desk. I pulled up the other chair so we could face each other.

I described her behavior and told her how concerned I was. I added that I thought her behavior might affect her success in the class.

This young, beautiful, 16-year-old girl looked me straight in the eye. She said quietly, "The reason I'm not cooperating with you is because I hate you."

I paused a minute, then answered, "That's all right. There are probably other students who don't like me, too." At this point, Sue burst into tears.

Handling the "I Hate You"

It took me a long time to understand something very crucial about handling students. They want their feelings accepted. By acknowledging Sue's statement without taking it as a personal attack, I was better able to cope with her problem. My behavior gave her a chance to come to terms with some of the extremely negative feelings she was experiencing.

I wish I could tell you that Sue and I had no more confrontations. It isn't true. She didn't always want to cooperate, but she did listen in class because she found that her feelings and thoughts were accepted.

Your Greatest Gift

Allowing students the priceless time to share their feelings is probably one of the greatest gifts a teacher can give. This sharing requires a climate of trust. It needs to be handled on a private, one-to-one basis. Your listening doesn't mean that you always agree. You're telling the young person, "It's okay. I accept you."

Denying Feelings Doesn't Work

I could have denied Sue's feelings. If I had answered, "Oh, you don't mean that," it probably would have ended any further genuine conversation between us.

What is Defiance?

When defiantly challenged, however, the teacher needs to respond with confidence. What is defiance? It's disobedience that occurs when a student knows what's expected, then does the opposite.

If Sue had decided to scream out in front of her peers, "I hate you. You can't make me do any work," my approach would have been different. Getting upset could have created a tense scene. An answer such as, "That's right. I can't force you to do anything," said in a calm tone would have prevented a counter-attack. Then I'd plan to meet with her during the last five minutes of class.

A Meeting Gives You the Advantage

Meeting with a student at the end of the class gives me the advantage. I have a chance to calm my own emotions. I can also plan what I'll say. It's important to remember that privacy is essential. I don't want the entire class hearing my words. It's unwise to confront an angry student when the entire class can listen. Why? Because the student becomes a performer and the audience will always root for the home team. A private or semi-private area for this type of conference within the classroom is a necessity.

The Student Conference

When managing young people, the student conference is a great tool. Let's go back to Sue. Remember, she is sitting in a comfortable chair at the back of my room. I am not sitting at my desk. Instead, I pulled up another chair so that we are close together and on the same eye-to-eye level.

Deal With Only One Behavior Time

During a conference, I must deal with only one misbehavior at a time. I need to decide whether I'll deal with Sue's "I hate you" or with her open refusal to do her work. I decide that the open defiance is the behavior I'll try to correct.

Briefly Describe the Misbehavior

My conference begins with my telling the student about the misbehavior. I let the student know how this affects me, then I try to encourage the student to behave correctly in the future.

Share Your Feelings

With Sue, I'd say something like, "I can't make you work in here. In the future it would be better if you sit quietly rather than disturb me as well as the class. It makes me feel bad when you refuse to do the work."

Then I wait. She needs to feel my unhappiness. Then I continue with, "You are an intelligent young lady. I'm sure this behavior won't recur."

11

After the Conference

Many times after a conference, the student thanks me, apologizes or both. When we meet students' anger with kindness and confidence, it reduces that anger somewhat.

Stay Physically Close

I find that physical closeness is important. What's important to the student is the contact with a calm, rational adult who says through his/her behavior, "I'm in charge. I'm in control of myself. Yes, you have a right to your feelings." It's a positive approach to discipline that brings results.

Remember that a successful conference is held the same day as the misbehavior. Limit your criticism to only one misbehavior. Keep your conversation short and reprimand only the student's actions, not his or her character.

You Make All the Difference

You are the teacher. You need to take control and be in charge of your classroom. It's a job you are being paid to do. No one can discipline as well as you can. No principal, dean or other school administrator can manage young people like you. You alone can make the difference in their behavior, in their lives.

Sending Students to the Office Doesn't Work

The old method of sending students to the office or to a "time-out" room doesn't work. Why? Because it puts the burden of correcting students' behavior on someone other than the teacher. Conferences with your students are effective. Students leave with their dignity and self-respect intact.

The Fool-Proof Conference

There are four steps to achieving the Fool-Proof Conference. In a private or semi-private setting:

1. Tell the student what he/she has done wrong.
2. Tell the student, "I feel badly when you ..."
3. Wait. Let the student feel your sincere unhappiness.
4. Using his/her name, make a closing, positive statement.

Summary:

1. *Listen to students' feelings.*
2. *When defiantly challenged, respond with confidence.*
3. *Remember to use the Fool-Proof Conference in a private or semi-private setting.*

3 Rules and Reality

Many new teachers spend a great deal of energy getting upset over little, annoying things students do.

In my first year, I wasn't called "Hitler" for nothing. Yet, we have to realize that some of the things students do aren't worth our concern. There's a big difference between aggravation and assault. And, there are motives behind all behavior.

Students Crave Attention

Kids crave our attention. It makes no difference if we're paying attention to them because they're good or bad. Sometimes it's impossible for a student to behave correctly because he or she may be into the pattern of getting attention through silly antics. The rascal demands our attention. However, some antics are best ignored. The very tricky part is knowing what to ignore.

I always end my teaching five minutes before the bell. These last few minutes are the students' free time. They guard this time religiously. They may sit with friends and visit. It gives me a chance to prepare for my next class or have a conference with a student. During this period, notes are passed or a paper wad doesn't quite hit the trash can. These behaviors aren't worthy of my concern. I may even hand back the paper wad and ask the student to try again. But I can't make a big deal of these small incidents.

The Shock Treatment

What else do kids do to attract attention? They use the shock treatment. It's easy. Students begin with swear words. The four-letter variety is most popular. They say the word, stand back, and then watch the teacher go crazy.

I rarely respond to swear words. If the swear word is directed at me personally, or if it's said in a loud tone so that the entire class hears, I handle the problem with a student conference. But an occasional swear word spoken in quiet conversation is not worth a confrontation.

Sometimes it's helpful to be preoccupied or pretend to be a little hard of hearing. Students who swear are looking for a reaction. Don't make the misbehavior pay. I find that if an individual becomes offensive with his/her language, a fellow classmate will correct him/her. Many times a reprimand from another student is much more effective.

Show and Tell

And what about shocking behavior? I have a friend who is a kindergarten teacher. One peaceful afternoon, her class was engaged in a game of Show and Tell. Two very bright, usually well-behaved youngsters gave her a surprise. When their turn came, they pulled down their shorts. My friend was young enough not to suffer a heart attack. In disciplining the boys, she discovered that one had dared the other. They were "benched" from recess for two weeks, and they didn't pull any more stunts. Obviously, this behavior could not be ignored.

Set Parameters for Behavior

One way to determine the difference between small annoyances and large problems is to set parameters for behavior. When I was a junior in high school, my parents told me I had no curfew. They said it didn't matter when I arrived home. Mostly they wanted to know where I was going and with whom. Guess what? I told dates that I had to be home by midnight. I wanted the security of a boundary, so I set my own.

Kids Need Boundaries

Our students need boundaries. They want to know what they can do in your classroom. They should know the rules before you try to enforce them. I have seen teachers give rules the first day of school and never mention them again.

Remind Students Often of the Rules

We need to remind students often of the parameters that we set. Classroom control is usually established within the first two weeks of school. This is the time to have all rules understood by students. Also, it's helpful to have reminders throughout the year. Situations change. Sometimes school rules change. So we have to regularly update our students on proper behavior.

Every grading period, I remind students of the rules and classroom policy. And prior to a specific activity, I will again remind students of proper behavior. For example, before a class discussion, I'll tell my students to respect and listen to the opinions of others.

Have No More Than Five Rules

One word of caution about rules. If we establish too many rules, we'll have a difficult time remembering them ourselves. I suggest no more than five rules, and I keep mine down to four. I'll share these with you a little later in this chapter.

Avoid Unenforceable Rules

Now that we've set some parameters, let's try to avoid impossible demands and unenforceable rules. During my first year, I had real problems getting students to come to class on time. I decided to solve the tardy problem. I simply made up an unenforceable rule. I told my class that anyone arriving late would receive an "F" for the day. Doesn't that have a nice ring to it?

An "F" for the Day

My students told me that this rule was grossly unfair. Of course, I didn't listen to them. Then, my principal came to see me. He informed me that I couldn't fail a kid because of behavior. I was indignant. I thought I had all the answers.

My problem was that I had set up a rule that couldn't be enforced. It was unfair. Students coming to class late was a small problem. But it needed a solution.

Find out if the tardy policy at your school works. If it doesn't come up with another plan that will be effective, or use mine.

The Bell Quiz

During the first five minutes of class, I give a daily quiz. The questions are easy. They may include a review of the homework or the previous day's lesson. Guess what happens when a student is tardy? He misses the quiz. That's a zero. My students are bright. They soon discover it's better to be on time.

Before you establish a new class rule, check with the experienced teachers or with the office. It's courteous and smart. Then you're covered if a student questions your new policy.

Avoid "Teacher Talk"

While we're avoiding unenforceable rules, let's also avoid "teacher talk." You've heard "teacher talk." It's language that's dated and worthless. It includes phrases like, "Buckle down," "Behave yourself," and "Shape up." Students tune out the teacher who uses teacher talk.

I know one individual who uses this type of language all the time. And guess what reaction he gets from his students? Laughter. They imitate him. It's all fun and games in his classroom and, unfortunately, the teacher is the biggest joke.

Assertive Teachers Act

Assertive teachers act, they don't just react. And they avoid language that is meaningless. I promised to share my class rules with you.

My Classroom Rules
1. Everyone deserves respect.
2. Come to class prepared.
3. Do your best.
4. Have a winning attitude.

I like the last rule the best. Too many students as well as teachers come to school with a losing attitude. I remember one beautiful, sunny day I was walking down the hallway, and I said, "Good morning," to the teacher just ahead of me. He turned around and said, "You know, when I enter this place, I feel the gloom settle."

I don't have much patience with depression. If I felt this way, I'd get out of teaching. Can you imagine how this attitude makes his students feel? Someone once said that if you can't help students, then don't hurt them. Teachers can't afford to enter school defeated.

Bring Your Sunlight Inside
Ever watched elementary school students coming to school? Mom or Dad drop the children at the school gate. They wave good-bye and smile in the morning sunlight. Then they run to the classroom. It's a joy to see. Young children look with hope to each new day. Shouldn't teachers? Let's bring our happiness to school and share it with our students.

A Good Pillow Fight
One of my favorite commercials is produced by the Mormon Church. It shows three young girls (about age seven)

in a bedroom engaged in a pillow fight. Their laughter stops when the father opens the bedroom door. He yells in a rough voice, "Is there a pillow fight going on in here?" The ringleader looks guilty. She's about to say something. She holds a pillow firmly behind her back. A feather floats down in front of her face. It's a tense moment. Then the father says, "I sure would hate to miss a good pillow fight."

The moment was special for that father and his girls. Teachers get a lot of special moments -- special moments for true discipline based on understanding and love. Discipline has never been an easy task, but I think our young people are worth it, don't you?

Summary:

1. *Have no more than five rules.*
2. *Set parameters based on sense.*
3. *Avoid "teacher talk" and unenforceable rules.*
4. *Use the daily bell quiz.*
5. *Stay fluid and learn to laugh.*
6. *Each day is a fresh beginning.*

4 Reach for the Phone and Call Home

It helps us to remember that parents are allies, not enemies. They hold all sorts of keys to young people, car keys, boat keys and skate keys.

Sometimes all our good intentions and logical arguments go unheeded by the determined student. I've seen smart students refuse to write papers, read novels or turn in homework. Then I found the magical number and called home.

The Magical Number

Parents want their children to succeed in school. A quick conversation enlists their cooperation, but one word of caution. Don't call when you're upset or angry. Wait a day and call when you're calm and rational.

Remember the saying, "Don't be part of the problem, be part of the solution." Sometimes teachers get so involved with the students' problems, they become blind to the real solutions. But before I share some tips for the proper way to talk with parents, I'd like to give my strategies for getting students to achieve.

Wednesday Afternoon Detentions

Every Wednesday afternoon, I keep a regular detention. For forty-five minutes in my classroom, I meet with those who haven't turned in homework, haven't passed quizzes, etc.

The detention time is for discussing the problem with the student, and for doing the necessary work (for example, reading the book or writing the essay). As soon as the assignments are completed, the student may leave. It amazes me that just the threat of a detention gets work completed on time.

Students Don't Have the Right To Fail

I tell my students at the beginning of each year that they don't have *the right* to fail my class. However, Steve, a very bright boy, was determined to do just that. My tenth grade class was reading *The Scarlet Pimpernel*. It's a novel published about 1945 with the French Revolution as its backdrop. Steve informed me that he didn't like to read "old books." Also, he had no intention of reading what he called, *The Scarlet Pumpernickel*.

Steve's Reaction

I had a student conference with Steve. I cajoled, I threatened, but nothing worked. Then I reminded the class that anyone who failed the daily quiz would see me after school on Wednesday. Well, guess how Steve reacted? He yelled, "You can't do that!" He insisted that I give him a pass to the dean's office. Once there, he told the dean in no uncertain terms what unfair things were happening in Mrs. Fuery's class.

Check With Your Principal

Remember in an earlier chapter I mentioned checking with the administration before setting up class rules. I had visited the principal about my Wednesday detentions. And he was behind me 100 percent. Naturally, the deans were prepared when Steve stormed the office.

Steve's Detention

On Wednesday, he showed up right after school. I asked him to read the homework assignment and to write the next day's quiz. For each question I used, I gave him ten extra points. I also let him know that this would bring up some of his low test scores. Steve not only wrote ten great questions, but he wrote the correct answers, too. I used the entire test the next day. Steve received an "A" and proceeded to get high marks until we completed the book. Believe me, he was a much happier student.

Get Support

Yet it took more than just a detention to get Steve to work. It also took a call home. Prior to his staying for the detention, I reached Steve's mother.

I had two good reasons for calling his home. Steve's parents needed to be aware of the problem and my solution. Also, I wanted their support. If parents are aware of school work that's not complete, they can put pressure on their child.

Calling Parents Takes Practice

Calling a parent takes tact and practice. I try to reach parents either at work or at home. Six o'clock in the evening is my best calling time. I keep my conversation short and to the point. I was able to reach Steve's mom, and this is how I handled the conversation:

"Mrs. Smith, this is Carol Fuery. I'm Steve's first hour teacher. Steve hasn't been reading *The Scarlet Pimpernel*. I've scheduled an appointment to meet with your son this Wednesday afternoon. Is that okay with you? (I get the parent's permission, and I've never had a parent refuse.) Now I know that Steve is perfectly capable of doing the reading. I'm sure after Wednesday, I won't have any more problems with him."

My Conversation Follows a Set Pattern
   1. Identify yourself.
   2. State the problem and the solution.
   3. End the conversation.

At this point, the parent may wish to engage me in a sixteen-year history of Steve. I don't allow this to happen. "I have several more phone calls to make this evening. It has been good talking to you." Then, I hang up.

Parents work as hard as you do. They don't like getting "bad news" calls before they've had their evening meal. They also don't want a teacher calling and saying, "I just don't know what to do with Steve." Mrs. Smith is probably wondering the same thing.

In the parents' eyes, you are seen as the professional. So don't overburden the parents. Their job is difficult enough. They have this child a few more hours than you do. Try to solve your own problems. And that's exactly what this calling home strategy accomplishes. The parents are happy, I'm happy, and guess who wins -- our very special client, the student.

There is still another advantage to calling home: Occasionally a parent will go out into the community and spread the word about the caring teachers at your school.

"Did you know, they really are concerned with my Steve? Why, they even called me at home."

Summary:

1. Hold weekly detentions.
2. Call home.
3. Keep your conversation short and to the point.
4. Share a solution with parents.
5. Kids don't have the right to fail.
6. Create happy clients.

5 Secrets to Winning the Games Kids Play

Young people play all sorts of games with their teachers. Steve's little campaign against reading *The Scarlet Pimpemel* is just one example. His little power struggle is obvious.

Yet, most of the games kids play are extremely subtle. Teachers may be totally unaware that a game is being played at all. These hard-to-detect contests are the most treacherous.

A game is just a contest with certain rules. The players agree to these rules, and then one side tries to win. When caught in the web of a game, teachers give students rewards for bad behavior. We need to reduce the rewards and turn these solutions into positive contests.

You can win. But that's only going to happen if you realize that a game is in progress. My first year I lost many games. I don't want that to happen to you. Here are some common classroom games that you will see played by *real experts*. Let's make the games win-only propositions.

The "Looking Busy" Game

Students realize early that they can get away with anything if they just appear to be working. If they stay quiet and unnoticed, they won't have to do anything. It's a great avoidance ploy that wastes valuable time.

Teacher Strategy

1. I call it "my beat." I walk down rows of desks, making sure every student is on task. Many times I can help a student who may be doing an assignment incorrectly.

2. If you suspect a player, stand near the desk and ask quietly to see the completed work.

3. Sit in the back of the room. Use the time to observe. Don't grade papers. Just watch and see what students are really doing. It may shock you.

The "I Don't Understand" Game

This is a gem. I had a student who played it perfectly. No sooner had I given an assignment when Sara decided to shout, "But I don't understand!" This is an attention-getting game played by the insecure child. It can be frustrating to the concerned teacher. Before I caught on, I spent a lot of time repeating assignments. Remember that you're not a human tape recorder. There are ways to win this game.

Teacher Strategy

1. Give instructions one time. Tell the class in advance. Stick to it.
2. After the assignment is given, ask for someone to rephrase what has been said. This way, the student who is sincerely confused gets to hear the assignment again. Also, you get to double check your explanation.

3. Tell the class that you'll be walking around the room to answer specific questions and to check their completed work.
4. Allow a few moments for students to ask one another for help.

The "I Don't Have a Pencil, Book, Etc.," Game

This game gives the player a chance to avoid failure. The student reasons, "If I just give up and don't try, then I can't fail." This individual is most discouraged and feels inadequate. He/she may reason that it's better not to try than to be embarrassed or humiliated. This game drives the sane teacher crazy. And if the player can get the teacher angry or upset, he gets bonus points. The class laughs.

Teacher Strategy

1. Stay calm. The easy solution is to provide the tools. Then the student has no excuse for not working.
2. You may decide to ask another student to share the missing item. Thank the student.
3. For the student who "forgets" on a regular basis, I schedule an after-school detention or a student conference. At the conference, I tell the student, "It bothers me when you don't bring your book to class. How do you feel about that? Is there anything we could do together to help this situation?"
   These statements let the student know that we share a problem. I've had students come up with terrific solutions. One boy decided to leave his pencil in my desk drawer for the entire year. It was amazing how well this strategy worked.

The "I Hate This Class" Game

This game defeats and destroys the teacher. It can cut like a stiletto only if we fail to read the unspoken message. Its other forms include:

"This is dumb."
"Why do we have to do this?"
"All we get are stupid assignments in this class."

All these statements cover real feelings. If a student could express his emotions, he would say, "This threatens me. I'm afraid I'll fail. I'm afraid to try."

Teacher Strategy

1. Use active listening. Rephrase what is said. "That was a complicated assignment. It's tough getting started." May open the avenue to a student's feelings. You may discover the real reasons for the negative remarks.
2. Make encouraging statements like, "If you let me see how much homework you have completed, I may be able to give partial credit."
3. A defensive attitude fails. Listen for the discouragement. Don't take the student's comments as a personal attack on your teaching. Active listening will make you a winner.

So now you have my secrets for win-only sports within the classroom. Keep in mind that teachers can not afford to become defeated by undetected games. Good playing!

Summary:

1. Kids are active game players.
2. Don't get trapped in the games:
  • *Looking Busy*
  • *I Don't Understand*
  • *I Don't Have A Pencil*
  • *I Hate This Class*
3. Reduce the reward for bad behavior.
4. Games camouflage real fears.
5. Listen for the silent messages.
6. Walk "your beat."
7. Stay calm.
8. Use active listening.

6 Stress: The Beautiful and the Ugly

Knowing about the games kids play helps us do a better job in our classrooms. Sometimes admitting there's a problem is the first step to getting it resolved.

When I began teaching, I developed a tough mask. Do you think I had a problem? Of course. Do you think I admitted it? No! I had myself convinced the students were at fault.

Sometimes we also ignore the stress that managing 150 students per day creates. And stress, especially unrelieved stress, can cause a myriad of problems.

But there's the beautiful and the ugly sides of stress. We need to decide how much stress is beneficial in helping us lead exciting and stimulating lives. Then we need to learn how to handle and manage the stress that causes us physical problems. Sometimes it's a fine line to draw.

First, let's look at beautiful stress.

Opening Night at the Community Theatre

When I became involved with a community theatre, I was the producer of a play. I was in charge of about ten people.

On opening night, I was wringing my hands as well as everyone else's. A friend was backstage snapping photos. One of these pictures is memorable. It shows the female lead with her head bowed, her face registering total fear. She's holding hands with her male counterpart who looks much the same. These two

31

had worked for six weeks and now, six minutes before going on stage, they were in the throes of total terror. You may wonder why anyone would willingly go on stage before 300 people. Well, the answer was in their faces at the end of the show. The audience's response made their stress all worthwhile.

A third actor, on stage for the first time, had a similar experience. When he was selected for the part, he told the director that because of sheer fright, he immediately learned all his lines. The fear and stress forced him to do the memory work required. He perfected his part and became the absolute villain. He nearly stole the show.

Beautiful Stress

When is stress beautiful? Is it when, as a result of our pains, we get rich? My cast wasn't paid a cent. No, it's when the stressful situation brings a psychological reward. Once we succeed, we know it was worth the pain.

Another actor, close to 70, had a tough time at the rehearsals with one scene. But before the eyes of an audience, he did his part perfectly. At the close of the show, he said he'd have to get his pacemaker recharged, but asked when he could perform again!

These players were high on the energy and enthusiasm that followed a successful show. Stress helped them achieve a goal.

Unrelieved Stress

So, when is stress bad for us? When it is unrelieved stress. That's the key. Here's how unrelieved stress occurs in the classroom.

When I feel threatened by a student, my body sends two messages to my brain: "You can stand and fight or run like hell." Psychologists call this the "fight or flight" mechanism. Now, principals wouldn't be too pleased if we started fleeing down the halls. So we learn to "fight."

Unrelieved Stress Equals Physical Pain

Our body creates stress which eventually leads to real physical pain. These pains include headaches, backaches, ulcers, frequent colds, high blood pressure, etc.

Are there teachers in your school who always have colds or headaches? Maybe instead of reaching for pills to solve problems, they'd be more successful trying to find the real causes.

Another sign that we're under stress is excess in anything. Chain smoking and heavy use of drugs (including alcohol) are sure signs that something is amiss in our lives. Perhaps we should examine the culprit and find the solution.

Unrelieved Stress Can Become Deadly

Unrelieved stress can be deadly. I knew one teacher who was in very bad emotional shape. He was experiencing a divorce. He taught the most difficult students in our school, and the students were ruthless. Combine this with a few physical problems and guess what happened? At age 32, he had a stroke. We almost lost him, but he's alive today and back in teaching. He has remarried and his life is now running smoothly. So did the stress cause the stroke? I doubt it, but I do think it was a contributing factor.

Changes Are Stressful

We know that heavy-duty life changes cause stress. I've seen men go bald or totally gray in the year after they divorced their wives. I've seen friends become addicted to Valium or lose excessive weight just because parents or grown children moved in with them.

We can't have stress-free lives. And we wouldn't want them. But it pays, once in a while, to examine what's really happening to us. We may need to get supportive friends or professionals to give guidance and help us solve the problems.

Do You Have a Stress-Prone Personality?

Perhaps because of our personalities, we create our own stresses. If I create my own discipline problems, then I'm also capable of creating my own stressful situations. Certain personality types are more stress-prone than others.

Psychologists have divided us into two personality types: Type A and Type B. Where do you fit in? Let's take a look and see if perhaps you're a Type A.

Read through the following questions and answer "yes" or "no." There's no right or wrong answer. No one is looking. Give it a try.

Stress Questions: Type A

1. Do you move and walk rapidly?
2. At lunch, are you the first one finished?
3. Are you impatient?
4. Do you find waiting in line intolerable?
5. Do you think or perform two or more tasks at the same time?
   For instance, do you drive the car and write a list of things to do, or empty the dishwasher and talk on the telephone?
6. Do you find that when talking with friends, you always want to bring the conversation to subjects that interest you? If you fail to accomplish this goal, do you pretend to listen while your thoughts are elsewhere?
7. During your time at home, do you feel guilty when you simply relax and don't work for several hours or days?
8. Do you continue to schedule more and more events in less and less time?
9. Do you feel that your success depends on getting things done quickly?

If you answered "yes" to six or more of these questions, then you're probably a Type A. But perhaps you answered "no" to seven or more. Now read and answer the following with a "yes" or "no."

Stress Questions: Type B

1. Do you check your watch infrequently?
2. As you walk, do you feel relaxed and unhurried?
3. Are you rarely impatient with the speed in which others complete work?
4. Are you rarely impatient with slow drivers?
5. Do you use the time away from work to relax?
6. At home, do you feel little guilt about not working?
7. Do you truly listen to what others are saying?
8. Do you feel that life has provided you with all the time you need?
9. Do you feel no real need to discuss your accomplishments unless the situation demands it?
10. Do you notice your environment? Do you appreciate the color of the sky or notice subtle changes in the weather?

Which Are You?

If you answered "yes" to six or more of these questions, then you're probably a Type B. Congratulations! Some of my best friends are Type B. If you fall somewhere in between, the next few paragraphs may help.

Type As try to achieve more and more in less and less time. They may be called "workaholics." They are more common than Type Bs. Type As may accomplish a great deal. The tendency to work excessively is not only socially accepted, but often praised.

Unfortunately, Type As also have a tendency to show hostility. Remember me as Hitler? Now that I look back on those days, I realize my own sense of time and urgency partly helped to create the hostility I felt.

Type As may not be hostile at school, but watch out for them in competitive sports. On the tennis court, the Type A may be the one to smash the ball right down the line.

Type As are time worriers. They are either running late or in a hurry. They hug your bumper, then roar past you in their frantic rush to God only-knows-where.

In contrast, Type Bs are rarely hurried. They may have the intelligence and ambition of the Type A, yet their drive to succeed gives them security and confidence. Type Bs make relaxed teachers.

Maybe you're a Type A. Perhaps you married one. What can be done to alleviate some of this self-imposed stress? I've listed some ways to help the Type A teacher reduce some of the pressure.

Stress Relief

1. Try to be in less of a hurry.

This is crucial. Try to change your daily schedule to eliminate as many unnecessary tasks as possible. If you have fewer things to do, you'll find more time.

2. Delegate to others.

To help you achieve the first item above, you need to delegate. Couldn't a student check your mailbox at the end of the day?

Along with delegating, you need to learn to say, "no." Sometimes we need to say "no" for our own protection. Remember that the word "no" is a complete sentence.

3. Avoid interruptions.

When you have a job to complete, avoid frequent interruptions. This means that during your planning period, find a place to hide. You'll get much more done.

4. Consider your words.

Type As have a tendency to create time shortages through excessive talk. I've seen work areas filled with teachers who spend the hour chatting. These same teachers complain that "There's not enough time." When we squander the minutes available to us, we feel more pressed for time. Don't talk yourself into a time shortage, and don't allow others to.

5. Work in a neat environment.

Sloppy classrooms create stress. The clutter around us does something to our minds. It reminds us of all the things we have yet to do, and it enhances our sense of time urgency. So, at the end of the day, clear your desk.

6. Create a few quiet moments daily.

This may take only five minutes, but it will do wonders for your mental state. Two comfortable chairs in my classroom make a wonderful sofa when pushed together. I lower the lights, lock the door, and close my eyes for about five minutes. I try to let my mind drift. It's amazing how refreshed I feel afterward. On days when I'm "too busy," I notice the difference. I miss my quiet moments.

7. Forget end-of-the day frenzy.

Avoid trying to get everything completed before you go home. Teaching school is unfinished business. You'll finish it when you die.

And while we're on the subject of the end of the day, try not to think of your car as your rocket home. I am fortunate to live on an island. The ride from school is about a half hour. Many days when I drive over one of the bridges leading home, I pull off the road and enjoy watching the bay and the pelicans. The other cars fly past me. I may be five minutes later than usual, but is it really that important?

8. Save your sanity with solitude.

Give yourself some time alone. I know this is tough if you teach all day, then go home to a young family. However, if you deny yourself this alone time, it's almost impossible for you to think about the changes in both your personality and your teaching style. If you can eliminate some of the activities in your life, maybe it will give you a chance to create some alone time.

My sanity saver is the beach. I walk almost every day and usually catch the sunset. It restores me and helps me face each new day with hope. Find *your* restorer.

9. Develop a sense of humor.

Earlier, I mentioned the hostility that goes along with the Type A personality. I had to admit I was indeed hostile to my students. Now I've learned how to handle it. I don't see every situation in the classroom as a direct challenge to my authority. I laugh at some of the crazy things kids do. Those same antics used to create excessive anger, but not any more.

I'm sure you've had students that you'd rather never see again. Students who seem to bring out the worst in your personality. There's not too much you can do about that, but there is something you can do about friends and relatives.

39

Cultivate people you enjoy. Type B's make good friends because they listen to conversations and have books they've had time to read. What a pleasure they are to be around.

Is there a family member who brings out the worst in you? If so, maybe this will be the year you skip the family reunion. It may be better to avoid contact than to put up with the stress.

Stress is a part of our teaching life. The more we know about our own personality, the better we'll be able to cope with the problems of stress. Let's not create our own pain.

Summary:

1. *It's okay to be a Type A.*
2. *Consider your words.*
3. *Create five minutes of quiet time.*
4. *Don't let sixth hour leave you in a frenzy.*
5. *Have a sanity saver that's drug free.*
6. *Surround yourself with supportive friends.*

7 Praise Person and Salesperson

Stress creates tension. And what happens to all that tension at the end of the school day? It stays inside you. But there are beneficial ways to relieve stress. The best is through exercise.

I know teachers who are avid joggers or who play tennis three afternoons a week. Others lift weights or play racquetball. As for me, I do aerobics, mainly because I like the way it makes me feel. Also, I'm in love with my teacher. He's tall, dark, and delicious. He has tan biceps, and he looks directly at me. "You're doing great," he tells me. "Keep it up. Don't stop now. You're beautiful."

Do you understand why I'm in love? He never says a discouraging word. He's cheerful and friendly. He really believes I can lift my legs and do a sit-up at the same time. What a guy!

Use Encouraging Words

If aerobic instructors can use praise, so can teachers. Too many schools are places where there's "never heard an encouraging word." Most classes are discouraged groups. Students would rather quit than try. Therefore, let's praise the class. Begin at the beginning of the year.

41

Opening Day: The First Day of School

I can never sleep the night before the first day of school. I don't know if it's the anticipation, the anxiety or what. I know kids don't sleep much either.

The first day of school is a lot like the opening night of a play. You don't know how you'll be received. Will the critics toss roses or throw rotten eggs?

Keep in mind that no matter how experienced you are, that first day is still difficult. It's like making love. Every time you make love to a new person, it's the first time. No wonder you're nervous! I don't think it's our job to scare kids on that first day. I do think it's time for some encouragement.

Opening Remarks

I begin my classes with the following First Day Speech:

"I'm Mrs. Fuery, your Senior English teacher. My name is pronounced 'Fury,' like the Plymouth Fury. But I have been called Mrs. Furry and Mrs. Ferry. So, anything that's close for this first couple of weeks, I'll answer to."
(I don't want my name to be a problem for them. They have enough to deal with.)

"I am really looking forward to this class because I heard such good reports from last year's teachers." *(Sometimes it pays to lie.)*
"I don't know why, but guidance always seems to bless me with some of the best students. You are part of that group, or you wouldn't be

sitting here in this room." *(Then I get an interesting reaction. The kids sit taller.)*

"Our subject is English Literature. It's fascinating. I may be asking you to write down for me what you know about this subject. If you write one word or nothing, then that's good. I'm here to teach you.

"I'll keep the homework to a minimum. You'll probably have assignments three or four nights per week. Sometimes I won't ask that you write your homework. It will involve reading the material or studying for a test.

"Also, you can expect short quizzes every day. Now, I know that sounds bad, but it's really not. It will be something 1 asked you to read or look over the night before. We probably will have a quiz by Wednesday or Thursday of this week because I want you to settle into school. Are there any questions?"

Questions Convey Fear

This is the time when a few brave souls will most likely voice some uncertainty and doubt. Listen to the questions and listen to the fears they convey.

During this question-and-answer time, kids will want to know if they can be successful in your class. It's important that they ask questions.

43

Then I continue:

"This is an entirely new year. And whether you realize it or not, you're an entirely new person. Don't tell me about last year. I don't care if you have failed three years of English at this school. That makes no difference to me. You're in my class. You can succeed here. In fact, it's my job to see that you do succeed. I don't like failure. It's my aim to see that each and every one of you does well.

"Now, I'd like to read to you some comments from last year's students." *(As a first-year teacher, you won't have any material from last year, but please borrow mine.)*

"The following comments came from a high school student at the end of her senior year. The question was, 'How did you feel at the beginning of the year, and how do you feel about this class now?'"

One student wrote:

"At the beginning of the year, I felt out of place and shy. I was really glad I sat by the door. I hated to read out loud, and I felt dumb and behind. I could have been degraded really early. Now I feel totally okay. No one seems to make me feel uneasy. I sit in the middle of the room and I love this seat more than the other one which is hard to believe. I love this class, and I love learning those neat poems we read."

44

Another student wrote:
"At the beginning of the year, my feeling was, Oh, God, not again. I came to this class with a poor attitude and wasn't willing to put forth or participate. Now I'm able to relax more, and I enjoy this class."

One who failed English the previous year explained:
"I hated it because I had a bad attitude about English. Now I don't mind class because I like the teacher, and I know I can make a good grade."

Ending My First Day Speech

"I want you to feel confident and secure. You can succeed. I'll do everything I can to make your graduation from high school a reality." My first day speech sets the tone for the rest of the year.

As you can see from my former students' comments, they felt inadequate and fearful. They needed a teacher who could convince them, "Yes, you can achieve."

Teachers Are Fearful, Too

The trouble is, teachers are fearful, too. Then it's impossible for them to be encouraging. When I began conducting workshops for teachers, I taught sessions for language arts instructors. I passed out small index cards. I asked the participants to write down their biggest problems with the teaching of poetry.

The responses I received indicated their fears.

"I'm scared of poetry myself."

"The hardest part is motivating students to begin the assignment and write the first word."

"My students don't feel sure they'll be able to do what is expected."

"Students give me an automatic, 'I can't.' The hardest part is getting them to turn work in."

It fascinates me that all the teachers were saying, basically, was that kids were afraid to try. So, it's the job of the teacher to convince the young person of his/her capabilities.

Teachers Have To Be Salespersons

Teachers have to be salespersons and praise persons. Your students can't achieve without your help. We aren't teaching a class of Apple computers. We can't ignore the real feelings of inadequacy and fear.

Sell Ideas First

Regardless of the subject, I have to first sell the idea. Then I must convince the students that what I'm asking them to do is worth their time.

Do Assignments, Too

An unwritten law among good teachers is that we never give an assignment to a student we wouldn't do ourselves.

I teach writing. I always do the assignment I've asked my students to produce. It provides the students with an example, and it also shows the class that I think the assignment is worthwhile.

Teacher Expectation Is Crucial

It helps to remember that we get exactly what we expect. Teacher expectation is crucial. This was shown clearly in a study done a while back called, "Pygmalion in the Classroom."

Are you familiar with the Greek myth Pygmalion? Pygmalion, an artist and sculptor, created a lovely statue. He was so enamored of his artwork that he couldn't live without her. So he prayed to a goddess who naturally gave the statue life.

Pygmalion in Your Classroom

Teachers do that for students. We create success stories based on what we believe to be each child's potential.

The Pygmalion study involved sending a group of college professors into an elementary school. The team told the teachers that they would test the students and determine who'd excel that year. They administered some old I.Q. test but threw the results away.

Next, they randomly marked lists of students' names. The professors returned the lists to the teachers with the assurance that each child's name that was marked would succeed beyond anything the teachers had imagined.

Self-Fulfilling Prophecy

Want to place bets on what happened? The kids whose names were tagged did exceptionally well. Why? Because teachers sincerely believed they could. It's a self-fulfilling prophecy.

One of my students recently made a comment in an essay about his favorite teacher. He wrote, "Mrs. Smith thought I was smarter than I was." If you expect success, tell your students often that they are capable. Then we will create Pygmalion stories of your own.

I'll never forget the day I told my ninth graders that I planned to have each student teach a poem to the class. Did I get applause? Are you kidding? It took a selling job, as most assignments that are worth doing.

Butch: Poetry in Motion

One young man, Butch, was a real problem. He didn't eat quiche or read poetry. And he wasn't about to get involved in this assignment.

Butch had a terrible attitude toward school. He came to school for sports. He was captain of at least three athletic teams and had a wonderful physique. He'd saunter slowly into class, five minutes late, and break girls' hearts. "Good-looking" was an understatement for Butch.

I needed to win him over because I knew the other students would follow his lead. Finally, after a two-day sales campaign, I convinced him to select a poem.

Butch and Benet

You'd never guess what he picked! He selected Stephen Benet's "The Skater of Ghost Lake." Now, it's an exciting poem but quite long. Butch took three days just copying it from the text. When he got up to present the poem to the class, he had memorized it . After he was finished, we gave him a standing ovation.

"Fail-Proof "Assignments

Part of my success in that ninth grade class was that I made the assignment "fail-proof." I told the class that if they really tried and presented the poem to the group, their lowest grade would be a "B." When teaching something difficult, I find it pays to give a high grade just for their effort.

Getting a group of students to read a poem is one thing, but getting them to write a poem, is a challenge. Just mention the word poetry and most kids are turned off.

100 Points for Effort

After a great deal of brainstorming and prewriting, I can get a class to turn in a poetry assignment by offering 100 points for effort. Regardless of the quality, the student will make 100 points just for turning in the paper.

Then I take these papers and look for about 6 or 8 exceptional poems. Most days I find that many in an average class; some days I'll find more. But, I don't just put the grade on the paper and hand it back. I praise the work.

Praise Students' Work

I begin with, "In my hands, I have some really good poems. They were written by your classmates. I won't identify who wrote these poems, but I just want you to hear what great poetry came from this group."

Then I share the poems with the class. Reluctant students shine when they realize I'm reading their poem. Sometimes they'll send a quick signal to a friend. It's like saying, "Hey that's mine!" I wish I could tell you the expressions on their faces. It makes teaching worthwhile.

Sharing Good Poems

I'll end this sharing session by implying that I couldn't possibly read all the good poems that were handed in. There's an added benefit I've discovered from this method. If a student wrote something that didn't quite come up to par with his classmates, he/she will sometimes ask to take the paper home and redo it.

I may also get some poorly written free verse. It doesn't matter, because their writing will improve eventually . And it will improve through encouragement, not discouragement.

I can reward kids even before I have read an essay or poem. For instance, I like to get my students working in class, then walk around the room to collect the homework. As I move from desk to desk, I say things like, "Jack, that's a good title." Or, "Mary, that's a neatly written poem."

On my 100-point assignments, I still may have a few students not turning in homework. It's easy to handle the student who leaves papers at home.

> "Jeff, you forgot yours. If you bring it in first
> thing tomorrow morning, I'll be able to give
> you 85 points. That's still a 'B'."

And Jeff always remembers the next day.

You have to work against student fear from day one to exam day. It's an endless struggle. Praise and encourage your students, and sell each and every day. If you perceive your classes as being successful, they will work for you. Sell yourself first, then sell the class.

You're the best. You deserve the best. Get in the classroom and play the winning game. Become a salesperson and a praise person. Then stand back and watch your kids excel.

Summary:

1. *Good teachers give praise.*
2. *Day one: Be firm and fair.*
3. *Break the fear cycle.*
4. *Create your own Pygmalion story.*
5. *Give an "A+" for effort.*
6. *Your high expectations are crucial.*
7. *Tell students that they're capable.*
8. *Give fail-proof assignments.*

8 Principals and Other VIPs

Guess who gets little praise? Who's the least understood and most criticized person in a school?

The leader, the principal.

How many times do you think teachers go to their principals with good-news stories? Principals receive complaints and gripes and very little else.

Want to change the trend? I sure do.

Once a week, I try to get into the principal's office. Sometimes I catch him at lunch. I share a few encouraging words. I discuss briefly how well my classes are doing and compliment him on a school event.

Guess how many other teachers do the same thing? Not many. Teachers see the principal's office as a dumping ground for their disasters.

Influencing a principal isn't always easy. Yet your school success depends upon a solid rapport with the women and men at the top.

If you want this job next year, you'd better establish yourself now. Here are some guidelines that guarantee that end-of-the-year contract.

Three Guidelines for Success and Job Security

1. Do something extra.

Find your sport and offer to coach it. Or volunteer to assist the person already doing the job. Super coaches need assistants. Be one.

2. Sponsor a club or create your own.

In a junior high school one year, a teacher I knew happened to love model airplanes. He organized a Model Airplane Club and discovered that the students loved the hobby, too.

One year I taught modeling to a group of seventh grade girls. After five weeks of training, my twelve models did a fashion show at a small, local dress shop. My principal was impressed with the confident young ladies. Five weeks hadn't turned ducklings into swans, but it sure helped.

My colleague who sponsored the airplane club had fun so did I. And so did our students. Sponsor or create a club based on your personal interests. Let it be known that you're willing to do a little beyond the normal day, and you'll win a place in the principal's heart .

3. Discover a problem and solve it.

Nationwide, there are difficulties with high school freshmen. They have the highest failure rate of any other group. Why? Lots of factors. Figure a way to get more students passing at your school and you've helped the principal with a problem. He or she won't forget that extra effort.

The School Family of VIPs

Now that you've made pals with the principal, what other people deserve your time and attention?

1. The Principal's Secretary

She's a key person. Usually, she knows more than any other individual at the school. She'll help you fill out countless county forms and guide you about school procedure. She does one more thing very well. She's your barometer to the principal.

When you and your significant other plan to spend a week in Hawaii, check with the school secretary. Don't just barge into the principal's office with your bikini and motel brochure in hand. It might not be the day to bother the boss. He/she may have experienced a sleepless night, or the ulcer is acting up again.

The secretary can be your ally, your solid guide, and your school friend. Win her confidence and learn what she can teach you.

2. The Custodian

Some teachers think that learning a custodian's name and actually having a conversation with one is beneath their dignity. However, custodians can be your biggest asset.

They get around the campus. They know what's going on. Who keeps your room in tip top shape, provides that new pencil sharpener, or that great, long worktable? It's not going to be the administrator in charge of maintenance. No, it's your janitor. The one who cares for your classroom as you do.

My all-time favorite custodian was Alfred. He was in his late 60's and a real treat. Alfred knew I cared about my classroom. My students and I left a neat room at the end of the day. I wrote him thank you notes.

54

After a summer in Italy, he brought me back an expensive bottle of wine. I cared for him, and he cared for me. And I never needed anything.

Who else is essential for making it through year one?

3. The School Counselor

Select a good one through recommendations from your experienced friends and use him or her. I adopted mine many years ago.

He's 60 and thinks like a 30 year old. Everyone loves him, including me, my kids, the teachers, and the parents. He relates well to all ages, and doesn't spend hours solving problems. He's been a source of strength and knowledge.

A counselor can help you get through the changes. There will be many, in both your personal and school lives. Anyone who has been through a major life change, such as this new job, a marriage, a divorce, or a baby, knows what I'm talking about.

Sometimes, sympathetic friends just aren't enough. We need the advice of an expert to unravel the mysteries of students' and our own behavior. Find a counselor you can trust and get their expert help. It's well worth your time.

4. The Librarian

An angel without wings. They are helpful individuals. The librarians I have known have been reliable, generous, and kind.

Most librarians will do anything to make your teaching easier. They find research materials when you're working on a master's degree, and provide guidance when your kids are in the library. And they are avid readers. Get to know your librarian, and you will have the sources of the world at your fingertips.

5. Mentors

I've had many. I began teaching career in a hot, dry Texas town. Mrs. Dancy was my oasis. I saw her every day during sixth hour. I shared her classroom, and she shared my grief. She listened to my "first year" tales of horror, and she gave me hope. She encouraged me and offered sound advice. She cared. As department head, she taught before I was born. She smiled a lot. Find a Mrs. Dancy. You deserve one.

Don't isolate yourself behind a wall of papers or books. Get out and mingle. Get to know your foes and your friends. And don't restrict your sphere.

Even after many years in this profession, I still have mentors and strong friends to whom I can turn. Sometimes we get in over our heads, and it takes a strong friend to throw that ring buoy.

True Confessions

Want to hear a true confession? One day at a principal's committee meeting, I made a bad judgment call.

I raised my hand when I should have tied it behind my back. I was asked to chair a year-long school project, and like an idiot I said, "Yes."

The job was unbelievable. I had the responsibility of an administrator but without the pay or the power. The project took enormous time away from my classroom. I knew little about what I was doing, and I learned that I was crazy to have ever accepted the position. The people who told me, "We'll give you lots of help," were the same ones who never showed up for meetings. Talk about stress! I had lots of it.

It wasn't pleasant, but guess what saved my brain? A rock. Yes, my Rock of Gibraltar, colleague Louise. She was a steady and reliable friend. She helped me through each crisis as it developed. And if it hadn't been for her, they would have wrapped me in one of those funny white jackets with the long arms.

Find people to help you. Realize that you'll make mistakes along the way. But you'll learn plenty. Do I regret taking on the project? Not really. It taught me more than any psychology class about leading people, and it gave me a fresh perspective on life. Would I do it again? Do you see my hand raised?

Summary:

1. Do something extra.
2. Win the principal.
3. Secretaries are super allies.
4. Custodians care.
5. Mingle with mentors.
6. Find friends.
7. Don't do this job alone.

9 Dressing for Success

You're the teacher. Dress to succeed. Someone once said you should dress for the position you want. I always figured that one day I'd be a principal, so I gave up my blue jeans and sandals a long time ago.

Now, I may not be as comfortable as my casual colleagues, but my suits say something about my attitude.

Wear Business Attire

I take teaching seriously; I take myself seriously. My students love my business suits and blazers. Before I even open my mouth, I command respect in the classroom.

I recently had a representative from a business college visit my students. She was dressed in a suit. When I complimented her appearance, she shared something with me.

When she started at the business college several years before, she purchased two suits. On days when the suits were at the cleaners, she wore dresses for her school visits. She soon discovered that a dress lacked the impact and authority of a suit. Students misbehaved.

Establish Credibility With Clothing

Since her talks lasted only 55 minutes, she had to establish herself quickly. She discovered that suits carried the power that she needed. The wrong clothes can definitely hurt us.

The Sweater Teacher

Several years back, an administrator at our school hired a man to teach math. Unfortunately, this individual was employed over the telephone. What a mistake. When he showed up for work the first day, we were dismayed.

He looked like a refugee from a mental institution. He wore a long, gray, droopy sweater. And it was summertime in Florida. He was as thin as a toothpick, and I don't think he washed his hair all year. That sweater was his badge. He continued to wear it every day.

The kids made fun of him. He had absolutely no classroom control, and I'm surprised that he lasted a year. His contract wasn't renewed in June.

Maybe underneath the sloppy appearance was a man with real talent. Trouble is, the students judged his appearance.

He didn't have a chance. He didn't give himself a chance because he wore clothes which lowered his esteem in the eyes of students and adults.

Clothes -- Your Easy Hurdle

As a first year teacher, you will have many obstacles to face. Your clothes should be the easy hurdle. Dress the part of the teacher. Wear a suit, a blazer, dress trousers, etc. Cultivate a business look. Leave your college gear for weekend parties with friends.

School is not the place for blue jeans. There's a really good reason for this.

What's the number one look around the country for young people? It's jeans. Whether you're in a small Texas farming town or a Boston suburb, jeans are the symbol for the young.

As the teacher, the first thing you want to do is establish yourself. You do this initially by means of clothes you select. Look at the principal and other administrators. You won't see jeans. You will see ties and suits or blouses and blazers.

Your Classroom Presence

Experienced teachers have what I call "presence" in the classroom. They fill up a room with authority. Their glances can kill and correct behavior.

During your first year, you'll be establishing that presence. Some teachers can establish this power through weight or height alone.

I'm lucky. I'm 5 feet 9 inches tall, and with heels that means I'm close to six feet. I teach the big guys. Some are well over 6 feet tall. When I ask them to come to class, I sometimes look up. That first year was scary. The fact that the students did what I said almost shocked me.

If you're short, then you really need to depend on your clothes to add authority. A blazer or suit jacket adds weight and physical presence and will give you that extra edge you'll need.

Look Like an Authority Figure

If you doubt the power of clothes, I suggest you read one of the books about dressing for success. There's one for men and one for women. It's information you didn't get in college. And it's vital to dress the part, to dress for power and authority in the classroom.

How Important Is Color?

Color is essential. I have a friend who is in charge of school personnel for a large county. His job includes hiring as well as firing teachers. I happened to be in school one day where Bill, my friend, had a hearing on a teacher. The teacher was soon to be terminated. Guess how Bill was dressed? In a three-piece, black suit. His tall frame in the black suit created a powerful image.

Black has power, but other colors share this arena. They include medium gray, navy blue, dark brown, beige, steel gray, red, and camel. Select the colors that are right for you. Avoid colors like bright orange, green or purple. You don't want to look like a clown.

The exception occurs when one of these odd colors is your school color. Then you are safe with a green blazer or an orange jacket.

If you're a man and can't afford more than two suits, supplement your wardrobe with blazers. A white shirt and dark tie helps you create the business image, especially in the warmer, southern climates.

If you're a woman, my advice is to get two or three jackets that will go with a tailored dress. I enjoy my suits. I also get a lot of mileage from my blazers and skirts.

A Sexy Image Is Out

I don't take my jacket off in the classroom. Research shows that just a blouse and skirt creates a sexy image. I teach boys 17 and 18 years old. The last thing I want to do is turn my students on. I'm safe wearing business attire -- a skirt and tailored shirt and blazer. And unless the air conditioner isn't working, I keep my jacket on.

New Life, New Clothes

A friend of mine who teaches art in elementary school was recently going through the pain of a divorce. In the process, she made some drastic changes in her personal appearance. Because she taught art to small pupils with hands covered with glue and paint, Nancy wore old, faded blue jeans to class.

She was a young, attractive woman, but she always looked sloppy at school. She started dating a fellow teacher who sometimes surprised her by picking her up at the end of the school day. That's all it took to create a new look.

Nancy threw away her paint covered jeans and came to school in sharp suits and dresses with blazers. While teaching, she wrapped herself in a huge chef's apron. At the end of the day, she looked great. Her students noticed the change. She was given compliments from her little charges. And there's a happy ending to her story: She has since remarried and has been promoted. It pays to dress well.

Your Sharper Image

Clothes may not make the teacher, but they certainly help. Clothes can help you feel more powerful.

I have a confession to make. When I first started teaching, the miniskirt was the rage. I wore my skirts as short as my high school students did. The hems came up to my armpits. It was a thrill to watch me use the blackboard.

I had long, straight hair, and I sometimes didn't wear a bra. I was direct from California beach life, a free spirit right from college and headed for disaster in the classroom.

No one could have told me then that my style of dress had a detrimental effect on my teaching.

I truly believed that dressing in style was more important than dressing for work, but I learned.

Your Acceptance By Students

Students will accept you if you look as if you have some authority. If you dress like the students, it's tough to gain any kind of presence in the classroom.

Clothes should help your teaching. They should be an asset, another tool in your success kit.

Summary:

1. *Dress the part.*
2. *Look like a powerful teacher.*
3. *Select colors that carry impact.*
4. *Presence plus power equals authority.*
5. *Clothes are a tool in your success kit.*

10 Handle Rejection and Win Attention

While you're selecting a suit, there's something else you'll need: a rejection-proof shield. I have a friend who sells real estate. In Florida that's not too unusual. What is unusual about this person is that he gives workshops. He teaches his audiences not to *sell* real estate, but to *handle rejection.*

He is a miracle. He knows how to push aside resistance and roadblocks. He knows the secrets to winning clients over.

Your Students Are Your Clients

Think of your students as clients you're trying to win over, and don't allow another teacher to deter you from the attempt. Some of the most discouraged individuals are teachers. Don't allow an embittered, yet experienced, teacher get in the way on the path to motivating kids. Keep your shield handy.

Avoid Toxic Teachers

One year, my classroom was across the hall from the school's chronic complainer. This man was due to retire. He was filled with animosity. Unless he was saying something crude about the principal, I never saw him smile. He'd breathe garlic breath in my face and try to engage me in negative conversations almost daily.

In the beginning, I didn't realize what was happening. I just knew that after listening to him gripe, I was always in a bad mood. Then I figured out that he was discouraging me. From that point on, I avoided the man. Before class began, I'd stay in my classroom or visit another teacher. I refused to allow his negative attitude to invade my high spirits. You're the fresh, young face, the new teacher. Avoid those with toxic personalities.

Cultivate Jean Cheerful

While we're avoiding war-shocked veterans like Henry the Horrible, let's cultivate Jean Cheerful. Jean is a new teacher at my school. She'd taught school before but not on the high school level. She is energetic, enthusiastic, blonde and bubbly. She loves kids, and she loves her job. I'm lucky to share a planning period with this marvelous person. She is as busy as I am, and sometimes all we have is five minutes together. That's enough. She sends me into my next class with a smile.

Happy Teachers Are Willing To Share

One other advantage in cultivating happy teachers -- they are always willing to share teaching and discipline tips. They share encouraging words.

Now that we've cultivated encouragement, let's look at another aspect of this motivation game. It's called the "frantic antic." A frantic antic occurs when you don't plan for a student's predictable reaction. It is failing to anticipate.

Like driving defensively, if you don't watch for the highway patrol car or the blind tourist, you're in trouble. Remember that if anything can go wrong in a classroom, it usually will go wrong at the very worst time.

Combat Discouragement

When can you anticipate trouble? When you tell the class with a smile, "And now we'll study linear equations." When you give the due date for the 5,000-word term paper. When you announce that by Friday, each student must bring a collection of fifteen common insects. Be ready to combat the discouragement that most assignments will cause. But negative reactions aren't limited to just the students.

I've learned a lot through teaching teachers. Remember the fears expressed by teachers when they had to teach poetry? Teachers have the exact same fears as their students.

I have developed a two-step system for overcoming rejection and getting students motivated. It's successful whether you teach geography or general math. Give it a try. I guarantee that it works.

Two Steps to Overcoming Rejection
Step 1: Get the Negative First.

It clears the air. Before I'll teach a class of reluctant kids I ask my students how they feel about poetry. Their reactions are explosive. They make comments like, "It's hard to read," or "Poetry doesn't make any sense."

Maybe the kids aren't wrong after all. I have to agree with some of the statements. Poetry can be tricky. I may spend two or three minutes discussing the negatives. I always get a few students who say, "I love it." That's terrific! I've won some over without really trying.

Step 2: Do the Selling Job.

The ability to sell is crucial for successful motivation. Does this sound familiar? We did a chapter on selling, yet we still need to look at this essential skill.

Whether I'm teaching workshops or tenth graders, I have to sell the idea that what I'm teaching is worth the time it takes to learn.

There's more than one approach to successful sales. The main person who needs to be convinced is *you*. I know you can't write the course of study. You may be asked to teach something that doesn't exactly thrill you.

Convince Yourself: Review the Material

Spend a Saturday afternoon reviewing the material. You may decide to skip a section. Until you can convince yourself that what you're teaching is worthwhile, you'll never be able to convince a class.

If something is a waste of time, maybe you should stand up and say, "Hey, this doesn't work. I'm not going to teach it."

Try something the first year. Make a stand the second year. Why? You need to establish your credibility. Some areas we are forced to teach just might work much better than we had anticipated.

Sell Your Class

After I've convinced myself, then I need to sell the class. One way is to point out, in a most subtle manner, that the class lacks the knowledge you wish to impart.

Recently, we studied the Victorians in my English Literature course. I asked the students to list on a sheet of paper what they knew about the Victorian era.

Some kids were bright. They took two seconds and wrote one word: nothing. That was okay. I then asked them to share with the group any ideas they thought would tie in with the Victorians. The discussion lasted only a few minutes because the kids didn't really know anything about the subject.

Hold Their Attention

Now I had their attention. I kept their attention by saying something they could relate to. I immediately asked the class, "And, how would you like to be handed the English crown at the age of 18?"

I was using a definite technique. The kids had acknowledged their ignorance. Then I gave an anecdote about Queen Victoria. They were hooked.

After the topic is given, make the next thing that comes out of your mouth as interesting as possible.

When I told my classes about the English Romantic poets, I led the discussion with some information on Robert Burns. I told the group that he enjoyed strong wenches and strong brew. It woke up a few in the back row.

Some teachers give their students a short pretest. I think this is a wise move. Make the questions tough. Students need to realize that they don't have all the answers.

I heard a comment recently in my sixth hour English class. One girl asked, "Mrs. Fuery, if these writers are all so famous, how come we've never heard of them before?" Sometimes, the best answer is no answer at all. I didn't say anything. One boy shouted, "It's because we're ignorant."

When the Bell Rings, Start Class

Keep in mind that you are a salesperson. You have to sell the class. Start as soon as the bell rings. And do me a big favor. Promise me that you'll never take roll call at the beginning of the period.

Why? Because you'll lose the class. It's boring and predictable. Don't do it. There will be plenty of time to take attendance silently at the end of the period.

How else do you capture the class? Relate what you are teaching to their lives. Give a reason why they will need this information. "When you start college, you really should have this information." Or, "In the eighth grade, your teachers will expect you to know. . . etc."

Vary Your Approach

A successful salesperson varies the approach; so does a good teacher. You may want to write one word on the board and have the students discuss its meaning. Then lead into your lesson.

Sometimes I'll tell a funny story about my past. I was brought up with three brothers. They left me with a legacy of humorous stories that my students love. If I look hard enough, I can find a story or incident that relates to what I'm teaching. Why? It simply pays to get the class' attention. Without their interest, no learning will take place.

I knew one teacher who was famous for his puns. After a while, his students started making up their own. It kept his class lively and thinking. Good teachers will do anything to keep the students awake.

An English teacher that I had in high school once stood on the desk to give his lecture. And you'd better believe that we all listened. Vary your approach. Vary your routine.

Once a student of mine was discussing the school cafeteria. One lunch often served was the steakburger. The student commented, "They call it a steakburger on Monday, then, give it different names throughout the week. That way they can serve it every day."

Break away from the steakburger style. Wake up Willie who always sleeps. Give them a surprise. Make it funny. Vary the approach and your kids will beg for more.

Summary:

1. *Stay away from Horrible Harry.*
2. *Cultivate smiling teachers.*
3. *Vary your approach.*
4. *Change your style.*
5. *Motivation is a selling job.*
6. *Don't serve stale burgers every day.*

11 Self-Esteem Creates Champions

Now that you've mastered the art of winning attention, I have a question for you. If Walt Disney can create wonderlands from orange groves what do you think you can do with one student's self-esteem? Answer: Plenty. I've learned about self-esteem from every teacher I've met. Both the bad and the good.

Mrs. Sharp

I'll never forget my first grade teacher, Mrs. Sharp. She wasn't called Mrs. Sharp by accident. She didn't have fingernails, she had talons. She loved nothing better than to rake her nails over our misbehaving skulls. She kept my classmates and me in total fear. I was often in trouble. She made a lasting impression in my small brain. She did little for my self-esteem.

Dr. Swann

But then there was the college professor at Florida Atlantic University in Boca Raton, Florida, who I'll never forget. His name was Dr. Swann, and he thought I could write poetry. So I did. He was a gaunt, forgiving and gentle man. When I took poems to his office, I clutched my writing in one hand, my heart in the other.

He'd sit calmly reading my words while I stared at his shoes. He had long, leather shoes. And he never said a discouraging word. Dr. Swann loved my lines of poetry, and I loved Dr. Swann.

Thank you, teacher for encouraging my creativity and building my self-esteem. Dr. Swann knew that writing which was encouraged would eventually improve.

The Train Who Thought He Could

Remember the little train in childhood stories? The one who said, "I think I can." He was a small train, yet he had enormous self-esteem. The little guy struggled, and he kept saying, "I think I can." Did he make it? Of course. Yet no one mentions his teacher, who probably planted the successful idea in his little train's brain.

Self-esteem starts on the home front, then gets crushed or nourished at school. Mrs. Sharp was the exception to the rule that elementary teachers know how to nurture kids.

By the time students reach the seventh grade, teachers forget that kids are human. By the time they are in high school, we actually take great strides to lower the self-esteem of most teenagers.

We're especially tough on ninth graders. Nationwide, ninth graders have a rough time being successful in high school. I think the problems stem from a low self-concept.

In April, a colleague of mine asked her ninth graders to respond to the question, "How did you feel about school in September?"

"I felt like a dumb, little freshman."

"The upper classmen treated me like crap. "

"I felt like a little bug."

"I was alone. I felt as though I would be lost . . . and I was going to be the only one coming in late to every class, and everyone was looking at me."

"The shy ones like me were a little scared. The ones coming in with big mouths causing trouble knew they were popular and could make you look like crap."

"Feeling like crap," is not a terrific way to start high school. These kids were dealing with what they saw as reality. If we keep telling them they're dumb, that's what they become.

Not all the responses were negative. One student showed lots of self-esteem. He wrote, "I was thinking I was going to screw everything up, but I was never picked on. I knew everybody in the school. I mean my sister went here for four years."

What gave this last ninth grader confidence was the fact that he had friends at school. Group acceptance is crucial. Building on group self-esteem is a wonderful tool for the successful class and the successful teacher.

Developing Group Self-Esteem

To develop group self-esteem, we need to tell our students specific things. I tell my kids, "Cliques don't exist in this class. We're a group, a team, a good class. We respect one another's feelings."

Remind Frequently

I remind them of this philosophy throughout the year. Before a class discussion, we talk about respecting other students' opinions. Before we play a learning game, we talk about how rude it is to laugh at other people's mistakes, etc. Reminders do help kids. They help the group.

Praise Often

I also give group praise. Lots of times, I tell my students, "You are my favorites. I love teaching seniors." Or, "This is a first-class class. I look forward to this group every day." It may be sixth hour and the last period of the day, but I can still say I look forward to it.

Praise, praise and praise some more. You can't build this feeling overnight. It takes determined effort all year long.

Evaluations

But it's worth the work. Read what my seniors wrote on an evaluation of our class at the end of the year.

> "I feel our class is really close. It's easier on each of us to express our ideas because of our closeness. We care about each other."

> "The class climate is one of happiness. Everyone's not afraid to be themselves. I feel relaxed and at ease."

> "We're a family in here."

In August, I set out to build that "family feeling" of closeness. By May, it was there. That was my reward. How else can the teacher build group rapport?

Recognize the Individual

One way is through individual recognition. Most of the time, our good students get ignored. By sharing outstanding student papers, I honor the better writers. Members of the group feel a part of this success.

After a writing assignment, I'll collect and grade the papers, always looking for those four or five great ones.

Then the next day, I'll carry the papers into the room and tell my students, "Now, I'm holding in my hands some terrific essays. And they were all written by this class. I'll share with you some of the best papers, but I won't identify the students. After I'm through, perhaps you can tell me what made the writing so good."

Students really listen with an introduction like that. The author of each essay sits up taller and smiles. How much harder do you think that student will work for me the next time?

Mrs. Fuery's Honor Roll

Another tool to build both individual and group esteem is the "honor roll." No, I'm not talking about the grade point variety. All that is needed to get on my honor roll is a C average and all assignments turned in.

I list the students' names on a sheet of construction paper, then tape the list in a prominent location in the room. Students are really eager to see their names on the honor roll.

I had high school seniors concerned that their names were not on the list. They turned in work so that their names would appear on the honor roll. One mother called to say that it was the first time in 12 years that her son was on the "honor roll."

Send Good Letters Home

Sending letters home is another way to build self-esteem. I started sending "good letters" to parents. It didn't take much to get one of these gems. A student needed a "C" average or better. The letters worked like magic. The fact that they were all printed on ditto-blue didn't seem to make a difference.

And there was an added bonus. Parents loved the letters. They wrote back to me.

I've included my letters home at the end of this book.

My Parents Respond

Now, here are some responses from parents that made my spirits soar.

"What a nice surprise to receive a letter from school with good news. It was very thoughtful of you. We appreciate it very much. Teachers like you will make Mike's last year a pleasure. His father and I are proud of his progress this year. Thank you very much."

"We want to thank you for taking the time to tell us Mary's good points, for the first time in her school career. This is very unusual and very much appreciated. Thanks again."

The First Time

Because the first letter was designed to make it easy for the parents to respond, almost all did. It surprised me that so many parents felt that it was the "first time" the school had told them something good about their son or daughter.

I started by building a good class feeling, and ended by improving school/home public relations. It was such an easy task. Accent the positive and you will win over not just one student or parent, but an entire community.

If you want to win as a teacher, then build the self-esteem of the students. Build each individual and you build the group. Feed your students the "breakfast of champions." It's an investment in a child's future. They are worth it.

Summary:

1. *Kids need to hear, "You can succeed."*
2. *Strong groups create wonderful classes.*
3. *Encourage the positive.*
4. *Use kind words.*
5. *Send good news home.*
6. *Post an honor roll.*
7. *Feed their self-esteem, and make them champions.*

12 Finding More Time

Time is a lot like sex. We never think we get enough.
I hear teachers often complain, "There's just not enough time."
They are right in many ways. The problem isn't with time. It's with our *use* of time.

The minutes we have at school are precious. We feel the "time crunch" because we fail to use our in-school time well. Experiment with the following suggestions. They will help. Your time is your life. It's all you're going to get.

1. Create time at school.

Arrive 30 minutes early. Lock yourself in the classroom, or find a quiet corner in the library. Don't allow interruptions from students or teachers. Without distractions and with full concentration, you'll be amazed at how much you can accomplish in just 30 minutes.

2. Pack a lunch.

Take a light lunch and use part of the period as grading/ planning time. I can eat a sandwich in 10 minutes or less. I have 30 minutes for lunch. That gives me 20 minutes of quiet time to work.

3. Stay after school.

I hold my own detentions. I keep students after school to get caught up on makeup work, tests, etc. That extra hour once a week at the end of the day helps me, too. Believe me, it's better than taking the work home.

4. Use the grade scanner.

Most schools have them. It takes 5 minutes (or less) to grade 150 papers. Most companies will provide the machine at no charge if your department will order the answer sheets. Another advantage is the item-by-item account of each test question. It lets the teacher know if a specific skill has been learned by most of the students. It's a wonderful asset for the teacher.

5. Do student grading.

Research shows that the more tests you give, the more the students learn. Doesn't that make sense? I give daily quizzes. My students trade papers, and we grade them right in class. It's an effective learning tool that saves time.

6. Learn to share.

The year I taught English Literature for the first time, teaching was difficult. I had taken plenty of college courses but never taught the subject before. Did I get help? You'd better believe it.

Within any school and certainly within any county, there are many teachers doing what you're doing. Why not share your tests, handouts and assignments?

Don't keep a great idea, lesson or unit to yourself. Write it down. Send it to your state and national journals. Spread the word about your successful teaching.

7. Consider your prime time.

When is your best grading time? It's when you can get the most accomplished. Your prime time might be first thing in the morning or late in the evening. Experiment. Decide what's best for you.

8. Create weekly time blocks.

These are essential, especially at the beginning of the year. I reserve a Saturday morning or a Sunday afternoon for grading papers or for planning the week's lessons. I enjoy this time. I'm rested and can concentrate fully. Weekly time blocks are worthwhile. Decide ahead of time what needs to be accomplished. Then set a time limit and stick to it.

9. Create to-do lists.

When Charles Schwab was president of Bethlehem Steel, he called in a consultant to improve the company's output. He eventually paid $25,000 for the advice he called the most profitable he had ever followed. Here's the advice, which could improve your efficiency by 50 percent.

Before you start working, take out a blank sheet of paper. List the six most important tasks that you need to accomplish. Next, number them in order of importance. Look at item 1 and complete it. Then do item 2, and so on.

Don't worry if you can't complete the entire list. If you get one or two items done, you will have succeeded. Why? Because the most vital tasks were accomplished. If you do complete the list, write a new one. If you don't complete all the tasks, don't worry.

I like to write my list first thing in the morning. I sip coffee, enjoy the peace, and fill out my card. I wear suits to school, and I keep my index card in my pocket. I check off the items as they are accomplished.

This simple idea really works. With all the tasks facing teachers, it's easy to get overburdened. The list gives my work focus. Try it. You'll be surprised at the time it saves.

10. "What's the best use of my time, right now?"

Whenever I feel I'm trying to do too much, I ask myself, "What's the best use of my time right now?" It's a quick and efficient way to focus my minutes. Maybe it's time to pat the cat, chop the carrots, or grade the compositions. Ask yourself this question, and focus your time.

I've given you ten time management tips. Even if you only try one or two, I guarantee that you will improve the use of your time. After all, that's the only thing you can regulate.

Now, you'll notice that I didn't say, "Every day take tons of papers home." Lots of burned-out teachers cart home boxes of paperwork. I'm sure some papers never make it out of the car trunks. But the stack is always there -- a reminder of work left ungraded.

Procrastination comes in various disguises. It lowers self-esteem. You don't need a habit to lower yours. Don't defeat yourself by carrying home work you're too tired to grade.

I've seen excessive school work done at home cut into family relationships. How can you have time for your own family and friends, or even yourself, when you hide behind papers?

Good teachers have learned to manage their time. They use non-school hours in a productive way, refreshing themselves so they'll have the energy to do a great job in the classroom. A life isn't long enough. We don't have forever. We need to use our minutes well.

I have all the time there is. Why don't you?

Summary:

1. *Find time at school.*
2. *Hide. You'll get lots of work done.*
3. *Don't allow others to waste your time.*
4. *Share materials with colleagues.*
5. *Make daily to-do lists.*
6. *Prevent burnout - leave work at school.*

13 Successful Classroom Management

How is classroom management similar to sex? Fifty years ago, no one discussed the details. I've got some details and tips to make your classroom run smoothly. But first, let me share four situations which help create havoc in the best planned classes.

1. Keeping a locked door during school hours.

I never shut my door, much less, lock it. Why? The moment a door is shut and locked, a student will want in. All attention is then riveted on the person at the door. And guess who opens it? The teacher. You aren't being paid as a doorman. Leave the door open, and start class as soon as the bell rings.

2. Fussing about tardy kids.

Appreciate those who make it to class on time. They'll be the majority. Don't reward the late comers by reacting to their tardiness. When it comes to being on time, incentives work.

I start my daily quiz as soon as the bell rings. The quiz is four easy questions from last night's reading. Those arriving late miss the opportunity to get a good grade. I won't allow makeups.

Your Tardy Policy

Within the first two weeks, my tardy policy is set for the year and so is yours. Kids know it's a pain to be late to my class, and receive a zero on the quiz. They arrive on time.

After three tardies, students spend an hour after school with me. That gets them to class on time.

Don't allow a tardy student to interfere with your teaching. That just isn't fair to the majority.

3. Taking too long to settle down the class.

The first five minutes of class is crucial. The longer it takes to settle the class, the less learning takes place. That's why calling roll is out.

The quiz is a wonderful tool to get kids ready to learn. I also settle my classes by having students copy notes from the board, write in their journals, review last night's homework, copy a quote from the overhead projector, etc. Be creative. Get them quiet, fast. Save your sanity and target the learning.

4. Handing out classroom materials yourself.

I have seen otherwise excellent teachers passing out papers and distributing books. Those aren't the skills they taught you in college.

Your healthy, strong students can pick up the quiz, pass out the books, distribute handouts, and do just about anything. Ask them to help you. Ask them to help themselves. Younger kids love to work for the teacher. Students on the secondary level may act reluctant, but I know they enjoy the recognition. Enlist their cooperation.

Now that you've seen four ways to eliminate havoc, I'll share some tips on running a smooth class.

Training Your Students

When I see a new group of students walk into my classroom in August, I see a group who needs to be trained in my method of teaching. We are not being paid to repeat ourselves. Part of my classroom training includes giving students the answers (during that first week) to the two most frequently asked questions.

Question # 1: Where does this go?

The student wants to turn in a quiz, notes, an exam or an essay. A set of baskets placed in an area with smooth traffic flow is my answer.

I explain to my students during the first day of school that my desk is usually a disaster area. If a student were to put a paper down on my desk, we'd probably not locate it until July. Therefore, all work goes into these specially marked baskets near the front of the room.

Kids never have to ask because they're trained to turn all papers into this particular place. If they do ask, I simply point to the baskets. It saves many hassles.

Before I leave for the day, I pick up the papers. They go in a folder marked for that class. This prevents papers from "getting lost."

Question #2: Where do I get that handout?

As kids enter my classroom, they see a long, rectangular table. I introduce them to this table the first day. Students know to pick up folders, books, handouts, etc. Then, when the bell rings, we aren't scurrying around trying to figure what we need for the day.

The overhead projector or the chalkboard becomes my P.A. system. I station a student at the door and remind everyone to pick up the necessary items before the bell rings. Give the "problem student" this job.

The baskets for turning in papers and the table for distributing materials are both essential to the smooth running of my classes. But there's another very old-fashioned tool I've seen too many teachers overlook.

Seating Chart

It is designed with convenience and time in mind. From the first day, I direct my seniors to the seating chart posted at the front of the room. I keep one, and I make a xerox copy for my students. They complain at first, but they quickly adjust. I mix males and females and try to get kids out of cliques. I move all my students every nine weeks. It helps them get to know others, which is essential for their own learning.

Taking Roll Is Easy

The seating chart makes taking roll easy. I always take roll during the last five minutes of the period. It also helps me learn my students' names quickly.

Having a seating chart that first day is important. First, you don't have to embarrass a student by mispronouncing his or her name. Young kids haven't developed that tough skin. Put them in a seating chart from day one, and learn their names during the first few weeks. That seating chart will mark you as an organized teacher. Kids respect teachers who are ready to teach when school opens.

Your Policy Sheet

During the first week of school, I pass out my requirements. This is a policy sheet that covers the grading scale, the tardy rule, attendance, daily and weekly expectations, etc. This covers me. Kids put this information in their cumulative folders. I have left room at the bottom of the sheet for their signatures. If questioned, I ask them to look in their folders at the rules which by their signature indicates they've read the information. It's easy to enforce a rule if you are covered by a policy. It's impossible if you are not.

Your Makeup Policy

Another policy that's essential is a plan for makeup work. Most teachers don't have one. And, without a policy, kids return from an absence and head directly for the teacher. All of a sudden, you're popular.

This will cause problems. It has taken you about fifty-five minutes to teach the previous day's lesson. And, this student demands a full disclosure in two minutes. Not just any two minutes. No, this student wants your complete attention in those very hectic few minutes before class begins.

A No-Win Situation

Of course, you have been asked to do the impossible. Don't fall into the trap. It's a no-win situation. If you leave out any details, your good intentions will backfire. The student will blame you. A comment frequently heard from students is, "But you didn't tell me about that part of the assignment. "

After many years, I've finally devised a workable solution. Teachers have been carrying this obligation for too long. We need to shift some responsibility onto the students' shoulders.

Here's how I manage to put the burden of makeup work where it belongs. Sometime during the first week of school, I ask my students to write down the telephone numbers of any two class members.

Phone Mates

When they are absent, they simply call a friend from our class. This student will fill them in on what happened that day. Two numbers help in case one student can't be reached.

Upon his return, a student may still be confused about an assignment. I will gladly discuss the work and answer questions during the last five minutes of class time.

Makeup tests are handled during my weekly detentions. Trying to give a makeup test during class time is generally impossible. It puts too much pressure on the teacher. Better for the student to stay after school.

Skipping Test Days

Unless there's a real health problem, most students should be in class most of the time. But they aren't. I know one girl who skipped every day there was a test. By the end of the year, her teacher finally figured out the game. But it was too late to change the girl's behavior.

Some kids will skip to avoid taking a test or turning in a major assignment. Students figure that the makeup test will be easier. We really don't have time to create new tests each time students are absent.

Oral Makeup Tests

I usually give an oral makeup test. They are more difficult for the student and yet easier for me to grade. After one or two oral tests, it's amazing how my attendance improves on test days. Another big aid, not just for the student who is absent but for all my students, is the kids' mailboxes.

Mailboxes

The mailbox is a folder. By state law, I keep a writing folder on every student. In that convenient folder go tests, notes, quizzes, etc. Handouts for absent students also go into the "mailbox." When the individual returns, I don't have to stop what I'm doing to hunt down a missing paper. The student just checks the folder, his/her mailbox.

Successful classroom management depends upon you and your willingness to work out a strategy and a plan. Your students should be as informed about the plan within your classroom as you are. I have tried to provide you with some added arsenal for managing kids from that first day forward. For additional help on the first week of school, see the appendix, page 116.

Summary:

1. *Have a tardy policy.*
2. *Get kids started immediately.*
3. *Keep an in-basket for papers.*
4. *Consider mailboxes.*
5. *Try a seating chart.*
6. *Have a makeup policy.*

---

14 Routines and Russian Roulette

Routines help to give our lives security. With order and predictable patterns, students thrive.

Weekly tests and essay assignments, homework on specific nights, all help to establish some routines for learning. When students know what to expect, they feel secure.

And they have a right to know what we'll be teaching. Our lesson plans should not be kept as close as a Russian spy secret.

Good teachers put on the board the day's plan. This may consist of a list of four or five items.

When students walk through the door and ask, "What we doin' today?" All you have to do is point to the board and say, "That."

For the most part, lesson plans are useless sheets of paper, written in the latest educational jargon for others to read. I think they are a waste of time.

The Win-Every-Time Lesson Plan

Now, don't misunderstand me. I think planning is essential to good teaching. Yet, the best plans are simple. Here's my win-every-time lesson plan:

Tell the students what you'll be teaching.
Teach them.
Tell them what you taught.

90

The Two-Week Plan

I plan two weeks in advance. On Monday, I'll tell my students what will be covered that week. I like to give weekly tests on Thursday. The reason: good attendance on the middle days of the week - Tuesday, Wednesday and Thursday. More students (and teachers) are absent on Friday than any other day. Also, lots of teachers give tests on Fridays, and I like to be different.

Since students know about Thursday's test, it helps me focus the learning toward test day. Reviewing the material is an essential part of my lesson plan.

What Did You Learn?

I ask my students at the end of the period to complete the statements, "I learned . . ." or "I relearned . . ." I call on students in a non-specific order, and they share with the class. Most days I'm impressed with what they can recall from the lesson.

The next day, we will review this material through the five minute quiz. I have students change papers, and we grade them in class. The repetition helps kids remember.

Weekly Game: "Pass the Shell"

This is a review game that my kids beg to play. Start with a small item like a shell, stuffed animal, etc. From the student's point of view, the object of the game is to stay seated, and literally, pass the shell.

The game begins when I place the shell on a student's, let's say Nancy's, desk. Then, I ask her a question. If she answers correctly, then she passes the shell to the student sitting behind her. If, within a reasonable time, about thirty seconds, she can't answer or she gives an incorrect response, then she stands at the front of the room.

The person sitting behind Nancy is now responsible. He or she must answer the question or go to the front of the room, too. When my students have worked hard, I may have only four or five standing. If I give a really tough question then most of the class may be out front.

Once each student has been given a chance to answer a question, the shell goes to the group standing. If they can answer just one question, they'll be able to sit down. If they miss again, they remain standing.

Now, a few important rules make this game successful. There is no talking. If a student speaks out of turn, he or she stands at the front of the room. If a student who's standing talks, then it takes two correct answers before the student may sit down. Students have to listen because I won't repeat the question. Answers have to be loud enough to be heard, or they are considered incorrect.

Rules for Pass the Shell:
1. A question will be given one time.
2. Don't speak unless you're giving an answer.
3. Say your answer so that the entire class may hear.
4. Students who have answered incorrectly must stand in a line across the front of the room.

Usually we play the game a day before the test. I have even played it for ten minutes prior to the test. It works well for short quizzes as well as final exams. One senior was surprised by her final exam. Her comment was, "I can't believe it. I spent most of the last four class days standing during 'Pass the Shell.'" She had learned through the repetition of questions and answers.

Be prepared for the laughter. The students will have fun and they will be learning at the same time.

To be successful you'll also need an overall plan. It's not necessary for you to plan months in advance. A course guide or brief outline of the material to be studied throughout the year should be sufficient.

The Daily List

My daily lesson plan is a list, usually made after sixth period, of the material which I need to cover the next day. Make yours as detailed as you need for your style of teaching.

On a weekly basis, I write and post on a classroom wall a shortened version of the assignments we've covered. It helps those kids who are absent as well as those who fail to turn papers in on time. As you progress as a teacher, you will work out your own successful routines. And, you'll discover that they create secure environments where teachers and kids can thrive.

Summary:

1. List the day's plan.
2. Ask kids to share what they've learned.
3. Teach them the game - "Pass the Shell."
4. Post your weekly assignments.
5. Create your own routines.

15 Motivate, Invite Learning

All of us remember teachers who directed the learning to just a select few. These kids were bright. They were the "right answer machines" and some of us didn't like them too much.

They always had an arm waving frantically in the air. Many times they shouted out the answer before the rest of the class had heard the question. And what about the rest of the class? What about the silent, sullen students who tune out the teacher? What becomes of their learning?

Teachers have an obligation to get the reluctant interested in learning. How? Invite kids to learn. Here are some tips to help you accomplish that task.

6 Invitations to Learning

Invitation 1: Have the prepared desk.

It's amazing how much time can be wasted while students hunt for supplies. Desks must contain just the necessary pencil, notebook paper and book. Train your students. When the bell rings, they should be ready to learn. This takes work, especially at the start of the school year. Kids have developed some bad habits.

Students are accustomed to dawdling at the beginning of the period. Unfortunately, too many teachers still take roll. Let your class know that you expect only the necessary items on each desk. Otherwise you'll find walls of books between you and your students. As that bell rings give them meaningful work.

Invitation 2: Eyes on me.

It's amazing how many students don't want to took at the teacher. It's an avoidance game. Chances are that if they aren't looking at you, then they aren't listening either. One friend of mine had this to say about her students, "They don't look me in the eye. When I'm in front of the class lecturing, I might as well be sucking air."

This is a quiet rebellion. And you need to win the battle. I say the following to my students, "Give me your eyes. I'm not going to continue teaching until you look at me." I also tell them, "I teach each and every one of you personally. Even though this is a class, I'm your individual teacher." If they are to learn, kids need to focus on us.

Invitation 3: Stay in tune.

Sleeping, drawing or writing notes to friends are all unacceptable behaviors in my classroom. I let kids know this. Talking while I'm lecturing or while other students are teaching is also not allowed. I've seen excellent teachers allow students to have conversations while they are giving lectures. This is wrong. Most likely the kid talking will be the same one who fails the test. Don't allow students to tune you out.

Invitation 4: Give frequent pep talks.

Kids are easily discouraged. To overcome the gloom, I give short pep talks. I tell my classes things like, "Give me the next twenty-five minutes of your life, and I guarantee you'll make a good grade on tomorrow's test. " Or, "There's only two more days left in this week and it will be Saturday. Give me your attention now."

I also encourage through group praise. "This is a smart class, and I know you will do well on this essay assignment." On test day, I might say, "This feels like an A+ day to me." A few words of encouragement will lift the spirits of most students.

Invitation 5: Involve the entire class.

Following a certain order when asking a class questions ensures that each student will be called on. If a student uses the, "I don't know," response too frequently, it may be a way to shut out the teacher and avoid thinking. If used too often, I sit down with the student and we have a conference. The more kids participate, the more they learn. Get all your kids involved.

Invitation 6: Kids teaching kids.

I believe we do too much of the work. Students sit while we do all their thinking. They need a chance to be the experts, and to be the teachers. They can teach many lessons.

After a research paper, my students present their topics to the class. Also, I've had them select a poem from our textbook and teach it. The plan I have given them can work for any lesson you want taught.

Guide for the student teacher:
1. Grab the attention of the class.
2. Teach the lesson.
3. Ask at least five questions.
4. Then ask for volunteers or call students by name.
5. Give a quiz over the material.
6. Grade the quiz.

The Advantages

Students listen closely to their fellow classmates. Some otherwise reluctant kids will eagerly respond when another student teaches the lesson. It gives me a wonderful advantage. I sit in the back of the room and watch the dynamics of the class. My students learn by teaching each other, and I learn, too.

Comments From My Seniors

How do my seniors feel about becoming teachers and being the experts? One wrote this:

"By teaching the class I learned more than the subject matter. Teaching requires far more effort than being a student in the same class. When you prepare to teach the lesson, the learning increases. Teaching provides a superior learning experience. As a teacher, I realized that certain people presented discipline problems which were difficult to deal with. Playing student is easier, almost a passive position compared to teaching. The student teaching program as a whole enabled us, as students, to realistically view teaching first hand. I personally learned much from the experience."

Another student wrote:
"I learned that teachers also have to do homework on what they're going to teach. It takes a lot to get to know all the information before you can teach others about it. I had to learn more about the subject matter to teach it than to just know it for a test."

One last comment:
"With a teacher, it's the same person day in and day out. With the students teaching, it was exciting because it was a different person every ten minutes. I learned more than I probably would have if class were held in the regular way."

Let Your Students Teach

Don't be afraid to let your students teach one another. The attentive response to students teaching each other may surprise you. The quiz at the end of each student lesson kept my classes alert and well behaved. I had plenty of grades to record, and I felt the time was well spent.

The Silent Rebellion

While we're motivating kids through invitations and student teaching, we also need to be aware of the silent rebellion. Students who hand in late assignments during the first week of school, will also be the same kids barely passing at the end of the year. And it's always the same reason late -- papers.

Extra Credit for "On-Time" Papers

Some young people wish to sabotage their own chances of success. As I have said, I believe procrastination lowers self-esteem. Because late papers used to drive me crazy, I developed a very tough "late paper policy." All papers turned in late (after the due date) received a 50%. I have found, however, a better and more positive approach.

Extra credit given to papers which come in on time or early, works even better. I find students will do just about anything (short of murder) for extra points. Experiment and find out what method gets assignments turned in on time

We have an obligation to not only teach all the children entrusted in our care, but to help students with their own potential success. Motivation isn't easy. Inviting kids to learn is one of the keys to their successful future and ours as well.

Summary:

Invitations to learning --
1. Have the prepared desk.
2. Eyes on me.
3. Stay in tune.
4. Give frequent pep talks.
5. Involve the entire class.
6. Get kids teaching kids.

16 Seasons and Slumps

Just as a student's self-esteem is important, so is the teacher's. And our mental attitude is chiefly influenced by the seasons of teaching.

The Season of Hope

The months of August-September are the seasons of hope. Teachers and students are fresh and rested. Kids won't admit it, but they love shopping for new shoes and shirts. And they enjoy being back at school with their friends.

For us, the first week may be rough. But most experienced teachers who enjoy their jobs, are ready to be back in the classroom. I can always tell when it's August. I start thinking school, planning lessons and activities. I like to get into my classroom a day early to make the place livable because I want a comfortable classroom.

The First Slump

The first slump comes in October. Ever wonder why state conventions are held then? It's because of this first letdown. Try to attend your convention. It will do wonders for your morale. You'll learn new techniques. You'll grow. Don't miss this opportunity to help you through the first valley.

Next, comes November. That means Thanksgiving. I love spending turkey day on the beach instead of inside a kitchen. November moves quickly.

December is hectic. I enjoy school in December because the spirit of the holidays is everywhere. During this time, many of my non-teaching friends get about two days vacation. Teachers are lucky to get two wonderful weeks.

Watch Out for January

But, watch out. In comes January. January lasts forever. For one thing, money is usually tight. Many of us have spent our paychecks before we get them. Also, if your school is on a semester system, January means the midterms. My advice is to try and take a weekend vacation. Anticipate this slump. Be ready to revitalize your energy.

Spring Break and Crazy May

March and April flow. Everyone looks forward to that welcome Easter or spring break. The weather gets better. Then, comes May. Do me one favor. Don't decide to quit teaching based on the way you feel in May. Why? Because May is National Burn-Out Month in teaching.

There are lots of reasons why it's so tough. First, you're tired. Second, the kids are worn out, too. And third, those irritations you ignored in September have become horrid monsters.

The person in charge of discipline at your school does a brisk business in May. Everyone needs some rest, and, unfortunately, the earliest vacation is Memorial Day. There's a month or so left after that.

On the secondary level, exams put pressures on teachers and kids. The weather is almost perfect across the country, and the desire to skip becomes stronger. How do I survive? Ask my husband. He says next year, we eliminate May. We go right from

April to June. It is a proven fact, the longer you teach in June, the worse it becomes. And, probably June is the time the least learning occurs. Then, comes summer school. I think summer school is for masochists. Some of my friends swear by it. They tell me the kids are good, and the teaching, easier. I'm sure they're right. It's just not for me.

Your Performance

The seasons and months of the year do affect my performance in the classroom. So how do I cope? My best advice is to make plans to overcome the slumps. A friend of mine teaches science. She does a sex education unit in May. You can bet she has no trouble with discipline or attendance.

On the high school level, we give final exams during the last three days of school. I prepare my students by playing "Pass the Shell." It keeps everyone's attention and improves grades.

Get Out of Slumps

Even good teachers get burned out and bored. That just proves we're human. Just don't stay that way too long. How do we get out of a slump? We need to become the source of our own pleasure. We shouldn't become so busy that we neglect to care for ourselves.

Do One Pleasurable Thing

Try to do one pleasurable thing everyday. For me walking the beach and riding my bike are essential activities. When I eliminate those pleasures from my life, I feel it emotionally as well as physically. I can't expect the outside world to bring me relief from boredom. I create my own mental health by taking time to re-charge my energy.

When you need a sick day, please take it. Substitutes can manage kids beautifully. Stay home with a box of tissues. Don't go to school and spread your germs. Leave your worries and good lesson plans. Get your rest.

I know veteran teachers and administrators who brag about never taking a sick day. One friend of mine had accumulated thousands of dollars in sick leave. It was unfortunate that at the age of 52, he dropped dead from a heart attack.

Teacher Myths

I've taken you through the seasons and the slumps. Now I'd like to make you aware of teacher myths. One way to create a miserable slump is to hold onto these untruths.

Myths to make you miserable:

1. Every student must love and appreciate you.
2. Your principal must think you're the best thing since carrot cake.
3. You must be thoroughly competent in all aspects of teaching. If not, consider yourself unworthy.
4. You need to become emotionally involved and upset about your students' problems and failures.
5. Your happiness is caused by your students. You have little control over your emotional state.
6. Until the school can "get its act together and do what's right," you have no obligation to do the correct thing either.

Self-Generated Unhappiness

Much of our unhappiness is self-generated. It stems from irrational ideas. If you've held a few of these notions, then congratulations. You're part of the human race. Some teachers allow themselves to get discouraged because the school isn't being run the way they think it should. Even principals feel there are lots of things beyond their control.

Accept this fact. The classroom is your domain. Don't take on the problems of the system. If it makes you feel better, work on a project that will benefit the school. Don't allow yourself to feel unhappy about things you can't change.

Ever notice the little shell of indifference that seems to surround doctors and nurses? Maybe teachers need a little shell, a little edge of indifference to get through.

Part of my work involves giving seminars throughout the country. I meet and talk with all kinds of principals, teachers, students and parents. I've learned that every district/school is like a family. Each has problems to solve.

I've learned to survive by doing the best I can and letting the rest (those things I can't change) go. You can survive the seasons and the slumps of teaching. We all do. Be good to yourself. I know you're worth the investment.

Summary:

1. Accept the slumps of teaching and face reality.
2. Put pleasure in your life.
3. Beware of teacher myths.

104

17 Ch-Ch-Ch Changes

Experience is a wonderful teacher. Yet the knowledge from experience is not worth the pain unless we do one important thing. And that's change. Change will carve and correct us.

However, I know some teachers who have taught twenty years, but what they've really done is teach the same year twenty times. That's called making a rut instead of a road, and ruts don't go anywhere.

Each year, teaching is a whole new world. I have to adapt to that world, or I'll be destroyed by my efforts to keep things the same. I'll fail. All change is painful. There's no quick or simple solution.

Instigate Change

One very helpful way that I instigate change in my classroom is to get my students to write an evaluation of me. After I've read the evaluations and discovered what's bothering my class about my teaching style, then I work to improve myself.

Weak, fearful teachers don't want to hear what kids have to say about them. It takes confidence and courage to ask students to share their feelings with you. There may be from two to five students who will write a vicious comment. They may be seeking revenge by trying to hurt you. Throw away those evaluations and forget them. But, if you keep seeing the same comment repeated over and over again, then perhaps this is an area that needs work.

Rushing Through Material

In my second year of teaching, I discovered county curriculum guides. I felt obligated to cover a specific amount of material per week. Because of this I sometimes rushed my students through material that we should have spent more time on. As a result, the evaluations came in with comments that said I was moving too quickly.

I have since learned to slow down and take my time explaining material or going over a subject, even if we get "behind" in the guide. My students learning is more important than being on page 189 by December. When I slowed down, I was doing a better job. Their comments helped me to improve and do less, better.

Student Evaluations

My students wrote evaluations on me during year one, and they're still writing them today. They are a wonderful tool for improvement. I like to be evaluated once per nine weeks' grading period, just as my students are. Therefore, I'm evaluated in October, December, March and May. I keep the form simple. When they discover that I want them to evaluate me, my students rub their hands in delight. The evaluation they give me is much more important than my principal's. I consider them to be the experts on my teaching, and I especially want them to be honest. I tell them that I know my own faults, and I would very much like to improve.

Evaluation Questions:

- What do you like about this class?
- What do you hate about this class?
- What have you learned about yourself?
- What are the three most important class rules?
- What one thing in this classroom would you change?

I will answer the questions, too. Then I share my answers with the students, and see if we're working on the same wave length. I get some really interesting evaluations. The question about class rules helps me see the classroom through the students' eyes. I have found the evaluations encouraging. And keep in mind that your teaching will improve with experience.

Comments From My Seniors:

"Mrs. Fuery tries to advance us in English. We may not like what we're doing, but when we're through, we're proud of ourselves and the teacher. She changed a classroom of crazy students into a classroom of crazy smart students."

"I learned about myself that nothing is impossible. I know I can do anything."

"It's not too hard to give a talk in front of the class, and this made me aware of my confidence. I have learned I can write better than I thought."

"You know how to make learning fun. You act like you really care if we pass or not. Those two things make this class run much smoother."

"You relate well to students. You care about us
enough to keep on us about our work
(a rare thing in school today)."

"You always make sure the work gets done. And
that's good. A lot of teachers don't care one way
or another. You push the students until it gets done
right. I like that about your style."

The Sole Unit of Change

I think the last two comments are very important. Students
want to do well, and they need adults to encourage them to
succeed. In any school system, the sole unit of change is the
teacher. Superintendents and principals can't do it. The only one
who can make a change is you.

Teachers make all the difference.

The highest person in the school system is you. When
teachers move up to county office jobs, they lose sight of the
classroom. The classroom gives my life perspective. I'm proud to
be a teacher.

Other adults are surprised to hear that I love my job.
They're quick to relate a horror story of a cousin who got crushed
in the classroom. It was probably deserved. Forgive me.

Teaching Is For the Strong

Teaching is not for the faint-hearted, weak, indecisive.
Teaching is for the strong. And, do us all a favor. Don't complain
at parties or church socials. Don't tell others "Poor me, I'm a
teacher." It's been done before. It's out of style. Share your
sorrows with your intimates, but don't spread sad stories.

Learn to change what you can within the system. The biggest change will come within the school gate, within the classroom. The biggest change will come within you. Go into that classroom with conviction, and do your best.

Summary:

1. *Let kids evaluate you.*
2. *Learn all you can from student comments.*
3. *Concern yourself with the things you can change.*
4. *Don't be afraid of changes within yourself.*
5. *Say, "I'm a teacher" with pride.*

18 Beginning Your Winning Year

All labor has dignity. It doesn't matter if I'm sweeping floors or pulling weeds. I've been a teacher a long time. I've also done other jobs; however, I like teaching better.

Some members of our profession complain that they don't get any respect. But you get the respect you demand.

My grandmother was a teacher. She only went to the eighth grade. My grandfather was a superintendent all across Florida. He had the equivalent of a junior college degree. Did they command respect? You'd better believe it.

Your Attitude Toward Work

Education has nothing to do with dignity. Salary has nothing to do with dignity. Work and your attitude toward work has everything to do with it.

Take pride in what you can accomplish with the raw materials of young kids - that's what counts. Get them looking up to you. They're desperately seeking someone to respect. Students need an adult to admire. Be that adult. Be the teacher.

Let Nothing Hold You Back

All teachers give to kids even when we're less than perfect. Don't be afraid to make mistakes. Don't be afraid to experiment. Let nothing hold you back.

110

Open Classroom Discussions

During my first year, I had open class discussions on Fridays. The students picked the topics. And we had wonderful, rowdy sessions. Other teachers complained because there was so much "noise" coming from my classroom. The kids were excited and the discussions often heated, but we learned from one another.

The next year I discovered curriculum guides. I decided to change my ways. I became like everyone else. I cancelled Friday's discussions. I became more concerned with being on page 108 by December than relating to young people.

I had a visitor come see me. Tim was a former student. His family had moved to the next county. He'd skipped his afternoon classes just to catch one of my Friday discussions. He was amazed when I told him they didn't exist.

I was a second year vet. I was afraid. None of the other teachers complained about my rowdy classes anymore, and a part of me died.

Strive To Be Different

Don't lose sight of your ideals. Strive to be different. Other people and curriculum guides will say, "But you can't teach that. " Don't be afraid. The kids aren't. They so desperately need brave, good teachers. Good teachers they can relate to -- like you. Be the crazy teacher who really cares that kids learn.

Get kids to care. If they care about themselves, they have the opportunity to care about school, friends and family. If they don't care about themselves, then liking anything else is out of the question.

You're The Heart

The center of all school systems is not the bureaucracy that weighs us all down. The center and heart of the school is one teacher and one class. The tools are raw talent without much direction, without much hope. A child's future lies in your hands.

I've visited many schools. It doesn't make any difference if the school is surrounded by city factories and poverty or slick condos and cream colored cadillacs. Kids lack direction.

The only person who can give that direction is the teacher. Be the teacher the kids need to have. Tell them what's important because they really don't know. Share with them your values, your beliefs.

Be Brave and Make Mistakes

Curriculum guides gather cobwebs while kids die of boredom in classrooms across the country. Be brave. Make mistakes. Dare to be different.

Get your kids excited about algebra, insects or verbs. Be creative. And care. It makes no difference what you teach, the main thing is to teach. Teach what you know, and then you'll both know it. Pass on the wisdom of your years. Take my hand. I offer myself to you. Give yourself to the kids. That's what life is all about. Offering, sharing, giving. There's nothing else worth doing. Be the teacher who is *Winning Year One*.

Summary:

1. *Kids need adults to admire.*
2. *Strive to be different.*
3. *Win this year.*

Appendix

FIRST LETTER

October

Dear Parent or Guardian,

This is a friendly note to inform you that your "young person,"   has all writing assignments and other work in. It takes self discipline to keep up in my class. So many times we send notes home when there are deficiencies, and not when there is something to praise.

There is a saying, "Catch them doing something good," that is circulating among our schools. I look for the good, and I've found it in
With encouragement this pattern will continue.

Sincerely,
Carol Fuery

TEAR OFF AND SEND BOTTOM PORTION
TO MRS. FUERY

If you liked receiving this message, please write me a brief note on this portion. If you did something special for your "young person" because of his/her efforts, I'd enjoy knowing about it. Thank you for a minute of your time.

Student's name:

Note:

SECOND LETTER

November

Dear Parent or Guardian,

  This is a just another friendly note to let you know that   has successfully completed the first nine weeks of my English class. It is no small task to keep up with the reading, essays, tests and other work, and I am proud of his/her efforts.

  The English poet, John Donne, once wrote, "No man is an island entire of itself; every man is a piece of the continent, a part of the main . . ." Perhaps he was saying that we are not successful all by ourselves. School achievement depends upon your support, love and encouragement. I want you to know how much I appreciate your help in making this first quarter a success.

    Sincerely,
    Carol Fuery

Your First Week: Jump-Start Success

The first week of school sets the tone for the entire year. Yet sometimes the beginning of a school year is stressful, chaotic and confusing. Let's make your first school year the best ever. The following suggestions will not only help get you organized, but will help your students succeed from the first day forward.

Ways To Get Organized

1. Hand out boarding passes.

To make sure your students are in the correct room, post your name and room number both outside and inside your classroom. Wear a name tag. Stand at the door and greet your students with a smile. Say:

"Hello."

"Good morning."

"Your smile brightens my day."

"I'm happy you're here."

Do as the airlines do: Hand students boarding passes with their seat assignments. Using boarding passes eliminates calling roll. Have stick-on name tags filled out, first names only, on a table near the door. Ask students to wear these for two weeks.

Ask one early-arriving student to change the formal names on the tags to names the students prefer. Collect the name tags at the end of the period or the day.

2. Introduce yourself.

During your introduction, explain a few classroom procedures. Have students face you. If they face one another, you'll get the rolling of eyes and expressions that indicate disapproval. Say:

> "I'm your personal teacher. I teach each one of you. You're special to me. I'm glad you're here. I'm excited about this new school year."

3. Teach the classroom procedures.

Explain your tardy policy. Train students in your expectations. Encourage and reward students who come to class on time. On Fridays give special treats to students who have been punctual for class all week.

Three tardies equals one 30-minute detention. I've had students ask me, "How many tardies do I have?" They know they can be "legally late" twice in a six-week grading period. Remember that an unlocked door avoids drawing unnecessary attention to late-comers.

Use phone mates. During the first week, ask students to select two other classmates and exchange telephone numbers. After being absent, a student calls a phone mate to get the missed assignment.

Go over dismissal routines. Have a system for returning materials and gathering belongings. You'll have better discipline if you train students to leave a clean, orderly classroom.

Teach ways students can get help. Train students to ask one another for information. Whispering a question is an acceptable way to assist each other.

4. Teach the classroom rules.
1. Everyone deserves respect.
2. Come to class prepared.
3. Have a winning attitude.
4. Do your best.

Everyone deserves respect. Say:
"I respect myself as your teacher and I respect you as my students. I feel the teacher-student relationship is important. It lasts a lifetime. I still remember teachers who influenced my life. I'm grateful for the opportunity to help you be a success.

"This class is a friendly team. Some of your best friends will come from here. You are a member of this select team. As your leader, I won't allow another student in this class to make cutting remarks toward you. In this classroom, we support one another.

Come to class prepared. Say:
"When the bell rings, have a prepared desk. That means you need pencils, a pen and paper. I'll list the day's activities in the same place each day.

"As you entered the classroom, did you notice the table next to the door? It's important because your class notebooks, graded papers, textbooks, daily quiz papers and all make-up work are located there.

"Read the daily assignments, pick up what you need from this table and prepare your desk. When the bell rings, work begins."

Have a winning attitude. Say:
"A winning attitude is a strong, positive attitude that helps you rise above disappointments. A winning attitude means happiness is a choice. You decide if this is a good or a bad day. When you enter this room, you're where you belong. You're with teammates and friends. Leave your backpack of troubles outside the door."

Do your best. Say:
"As your teacher, I promise to do my best. Sometimes when I'm teaching or writing, I ask myself, 'Am I doing my best?' If the answer is 'No,' then I ask, 'What needs to be done?' I expect my students to do their best."

119

5. Use a pick-up table.

This is a rectangular table located near the door. As students enter they walk past this table. Before the bell rings, they pick up folders, graded papers, handouts, textbooks, etc. The table contains:

Red makeup folder
This bright, firecracker-red folder contains handouts, homework schedules and assignments.

Blue makeup log
This is an information notebook. Each week a student records the day's date plus two sentences about the classroom work. Students returning from an absence read about the missed assignments. If they have questions, they need to see the student who wrote the information. If they're still confused, ask them to meet with you during the last five minutes of class.

In-basket
All papers go into the in-basket on the pick-up table. Baskets are marked by class/subject.

6. Write daily flight plans

The overhead projector, computer screen, chalkboard or handout directs the day's assignments. Use no more than five phrases or short sentences. When a student asks, "What are we doing today?" Point and say, "That."

7. Give directions effectively

Center attention. Create order. Train students. Say:

"Please listen now. When my teacher words are in the air, they need to go directly into your mind. Your talking interrupts the flow. I'm in charge, so for now, my teacher words are more important than your student words."

Have students repeat directions.
Ask students to repeat a few basic directions.

8. Get students working immediately.

Even before the bell rings, start class. As soon as students enter your room, they need something engaging to do. Train your students the first day. How? Have an assignment on the board, a puzzle or riddle on a handout to pick up, an educational game in progress -- anything to focus the students.

Suggested assignments for the first week:
1. Ask students to fill out a Student Information Sheet (see an example at the close of this section, page124).
2. Have the class listen to an age-appropriate story.
3. Break the class into two-person teams and have students introduce their partners to the class.
4. Do any activity that keeps the students engaged.

If you are a secondary teacher, get a copy of your students' schedules. When you need to locate a student anytime they aren't with you, the information will be at your fingertips.

From the moment they arrive in your classroom, your students will know what procedures to follow. This eliminates many discipline problems.

Challenges inspire. We make a mistake if we tell students that they can do the assignments because the work is easy. Say:

> "The work I'll give you is difficult, yet I know you can do it. You're smart and capable. You'll be successful here today."

9. Learn your students' names.

Your goal is to know many names by the first week and all names by the end of the second week of school.

"One positive thing" activity. Have students introduce themselves to the class by giving their names and one positive thing that has happened to them in the last two weeks or two months.

The name game. Have students remove their name tags. Then have them name each person in their row, table or team. Ask a brave volunteer to give the first name of each class member. Try to do it yourself.

10. First-Day Reminders

Classrooms don't have to be perfect. You can be a great teacher with a less than perfect room.

Your bulletin boards can be bare. Ask the students to decorate the room with their art or writings. Bare walls soothe hyperactive kids.

Explain the rules thoroughly. Do this during the first two weeks of school. Hand them out like vitamins, a few a day. Then before any activities remind students about proper classroom behavior.

Learn the students' preferred names. The most important question on your Student Information Sheet is, "What name do you like to be called?" Use the student's preferred rather than his or her formal name. A sample Student Information Sheet appears on the next page.

Correct misbehavior immediately. Unless you plan to put up with inappropriate behavior all year long, correct students now.

Summary:

1. *Hand out boarding passes.*
2. *Introduce yourself.*
3. *Teach classroom procedures.*
4. *Teach classroom rules.*
5. *Use a pick-up table.*
6. *Write daily flight plans.*
7. *Give directions effectively.*
8. *Get students working immediately.*
9. *Learn your students' names.*

Student Information Sheet

Your Name: _____

The name you like to be called: _____

Parent or guardian _____

Place of their employment: _____

Parent/guardian's work telephone _____

List any brothers and/or sisters living at home with you.

Name: _____ Age: _____

Do you have brothers or sisters living elsewhere? If yes, explain.

_____

_____

What has happened in your life during the last two months?

_____

_____

What would you like for me, your teacher, to know about you? What do you hope to learn from this course?

_____

On the back write a few sentences on the following topics: List and describe your activities outside of school. Include your interests, sports or hobbies.

Write a short paragraph of five to eight sentences on a favorite TV show or movie.

Discipline Strategies For the Bored and Belligerent

On one of my trips to give a seminar in a rural area of Texas, I visited with a high school principal. Discipline in his school was not a problem. He told me that his students didn't need metal detectors, in-school suspensions or detentions.

A former football coach he said, "I set up relationships with my students. When they have injuries, I'm the one who tapes their ankles. I do it better than their coach. They tell me a lot while I'm taping an ankle."

This wise man develops trust with kids. Good discipline means you've created a bond with your students. The following strategies will help you improve that relationship.

1. Decide if this behavior is a problem.

Verify if a problem exists. Before you attempt to direct a student's behavior, ask the following:

What makes me angry ?
What's the real issue?
Who is responsible?
Who owns the problem?
What do I hope to accomplish?

125

About the student's behavior:

Is it causing physical harm?

Is it disrupting the learning process?

Does it create emotional reactions?

Is it related to a mental/physical condition?

Is it causing this student to be socially ostracized?

2. Give your comic the mike.

Are we developing another Jerry Seinfield? Perhaps. One of my sixth-hour students, Steve Ryan, was a terrific comedian. Because he often disrupted class, I came up with the following survival technique: I "gave him the microphone." Promising to keep his remarks short, he began the period with a joke or humorous statement.

Most of the time his stand-up comedy routine used up only two minutes of class time. He received the attention he craved in a positive way. We called these openings "Ryanisms." On days when Steve had nothing to say, we missed his humor.

3. Play the Ignoring Game.

To play this game, you must give absolutely no attention to the misbehaving student. You cannot respond by yelling at, looking at or talking to the student.

Select a student who doesn't get upset easily and ask him or her to demonstrate this discipline strategy with you. Tell the student that you'll be doing a variety of annoying behaviors. While ignoring you, the student continues working.

You've picked Rick. Stand close to him. Tug on his hair, step (lightly) on his foot, or pull at his jacket or shirt. Rick shouldn't respond. After two minutes, turn to the class and talk about your demonstration. Say:

> "Class, the purpose of this activity is to show behaviors that don't fit in a classroom. By responding to me with laughter or anger, Rick rewards my antics. Unless the behavior is physically harmful, try ignoring it."

Reward kids who are clever enough to ignore harmless behavior. Students trapped in the victim role now have another option.

4. Place your student in a box.

The "Kid-in-the-Box" game works well with elementary pupils. In the center of the room, draw an imaginary box around a desk. Tell the class that if a student misbehaves, he or she will sit in the box and work. Set a timer for five to ten minutes.

While the young person is in the box, other students pretend they can't see or hear him/her. This method gives the pupil lots of attention, but no strokes for misbehavior. Just like the ignoring game, we need the cooperation of the class.

5. Review class procedures frequently.

Before an activity, review the rules of proper conduct, anything that will help students "Do what's right." Call on students individually or have the class repeat the rules in unison. Review the consequences for disruptive behavior.

6. Give choices.

When giving an assignment, say: "We can play the review game 'Pass the Shell' or we can vote to review for the test in our three member teams. Which would you prefer?"

When reprimanding a student, offer him/her choices. One physical education teacher in Virginia told me about a second grader who had broken a class rule. The teacher told the youngster to run 100 yards to the water tower and back. This shy student refused. Now the teacher had a much worse problem -- open defiance. She later discovered that this child was afraid to run the distance alone. She learned to say:

"You have a choice. You can run to the water tower with a willing partner or you may choose to stay after school for ten minutes. What's your decision?"

Giving kids an opportunity to decide their punishment makes "doing the time" easier.

7. Use humor.

Humor helps to ease tension. Bevil Lindsey, a veteran elementary teacher in Silsbee, Texas, recommends singing a request to a child. This method softens the impact, eases tension and gets the point across without further aggravation. A child who is laughing is less likely to punch the teacher or a classmate.

Remember that humor is like changing a baby's wet diaper. It doesn't cause any permanent changes but it sure makes us feel better for a while.

8. Acknowledge discomfort.

Acknowledging students' discomfort shows them that you care. When the air-conditioner stops working on a hot September day, I tell my students:

"I know it's uncomfortable in here. I appreciate
your willingness to work under these less than
ideal conditions. It shows your strength and
maturity."

Take a hint from the airlines. Pilots apologize to their
passengers for turbulent weather. Even when it's not your fault,
sometimes it's perfectly okay to apologize.

9. Use the 60-second time-out.

From second graders to high school seniors, this method
saves your sanity. When a student has behaved inappropriately,
call him/her back to your desk. Here are the various ways you
can use this technique.

Elementary level

Option 1: Ask the student to count to 60 while holding
your hand, or have the student watch the second hand on the
clock.

Option 2: Another way to use this method is to isolate
the student in a time-out chair within the classroom. Explain that
the student can't return to the group until he/she comes up with
three better choices for the inappropriate behavior.

Secondary level

Option 1: Missing one minute of lunchtime away from
their friends, or staying after class one minute works miracles to
correct the misbehavior of middle and high school students. Ask
the student to come up with three better choices.

Option 2 Say:
> "I see you've decided to break a class rule. Tell me what rule you broke and what alternative behavior would have been more appropriate. You'll be dismissed as soon as you describe more acceptable behavior."

Option 3 Say something like this:
> "You have a choice. You have chosen to break the rule which is, 'Have a winning attitude.' What better choices could you make in the future?"

10. Be aware of your body positioning.

Never get frozen in one spot. Shift the front of the room. Talk and walk to the side or back of the room. Make your movements a natural part of your teaching. The moment you get physically close to them, watch your students' attention improve.

11. Control your anger with self talk.

Step 1: Prepare for conflict. Say to yourself:
"This may be rough, but I can handle anything. I'm in control and calm. I'll stick to the issues and not take anything personally. I won't argue. I know what to say and what to do."

Step 2: Cope with your physical response.
Remember the natural response to stress is to hold your breath. Keep breathing.
"I'm breathing deeply, relaxing my muscles. I'm calm and dealing with this conflict constructively. I'm in charge."

Step 3: When the conflict is resolved, say to yourself: "I'm proud of myself. I kept cool and collected. I stated my feelings without attacking or raising my voice. I'm doing better."

When conflict is unresolved, say to yourself: "I can relax. I won't take this personally. I did my best. I'll reward myself by thinking about something else."

Summary:

1. *Decide if this behavior is a problem.*
2. *Give your comic the mike.*
3. *Play the ignoring game.*
4. *Place a student in the box.*
5. *Review class procedures frequently.*
6. *Give choices.*
7. *Use humor.*
8. *Acknowledge discomfort.*
9. *Use the 60 second time-out.*
10. *Be aware of your body positioning.*
11. *Control your anger with self-talk.*

This section is from the new book, ***Discipline Strategies for the Bored, Belligerent and Ballistic.*** For ordering information, call (800-330-3459).

Communicate And Connect With Kids

Biologist Lewis Thomas wrote that nature's great law of all living things is not the survival of the fittest, but the principle of cooperation. He explains that plants and animals survive not by defeating their neighbors in the competition for food and light, but by learning to live with their neighbors in such a way that all prosper.

Connecting and communicating with students means that we're given a chance to teach. The following nine techniques may help you with your special clients, your students.

1. Use "I Messages "

"I messages" help to get your point across without making students feel defensive. Here's an example:

"... I feel...when you ... because..."

I feel X -- a feeling, not an opinion
When you Y -- observable behavior
Because Z -- an observable consequence

This structure:
Describes, labels and avoids teacher talk. The student knows consequences of his/her behavior.

For example: "Bryan, I feel angry when you pull your jacket over your head and sleep in my third hour class . Because you're missing the lesson, you may not pass Thursday's test."

"Connie, I feel uncomfortable when you punch your teammate because his crying upsets others."

2. Use small talk.

Small talk or casual conversation helps you connect with students in a positive way. It creates emotional involvement; it shows kids you care about them and helps establish and maintain the teacher/student relationship. Before class, during lunch, after school are good times to catch a few minutes of conversation.

During the first week of school, have students fill out a Student Information Sheet, See Appendix A. Beside each student's name in the gradebook jot down the home telephone and work numbers. Add one or two words that might ignite a conversation between you and the student.

3. Invite kids to talk about feelings.

First, respond to feelings, then to facts. When a student is angry, frightened or frustrated saying, "Calm down, calm down!" doesn't work. Say instead:

"You seem quite upset."
"Someone must have done something awful to
  get you this excited."
"Want to talk about what's bothering you?"

4. Try the Sweet and Sour Approach.

When you need to criticize a student, give three pluses then the minus. Express three sincere compliments before your first negative comment. The compliments get the student's attention and makes him/her more willing to listen to what you have to say. Such as:

> "Mary, I really enjoy your energy, enthusiasm and willingness to share. However, yesterday your constant talking disrupting our lesson. Is there any way you might behave differently?"

5. Always provide face-saving comments.

Adults as well as children need a way to save face. You can do it using phrases like:

> "It's easy to get confused."
> "I understand why you're so upset."
> "The details make this difficult."

6. Use silence.

Pausing before you respond to a student's misbehavior gives you time to reflect. Everyone hates a void so we rush to fill in the silent spaces. A quiet, calm silence can work to your advantage.

7. Match your words to your body language.

Smiling when discussing a tough class assignment gives the wrong message. Match your facial expressions to your words.

8. Invite an angry student to sit.

We have the most resistance while we are standing. I keep a rocking chair in my classroom. It's difficult to rock back and forth and stay angry for long.

9. Handle a student's insults.

Don't confront or make threats.

Use conversation. Discretion and diplomacy are powerful tools. Expressing anger may be the worst thing you can do. Resist impulsive behavior. Would a conciliatory or humorous remark take the heat from the exchange?

Tell the student that anger or insults won't have the desired effect. Say something like:

"Jeff, yelling and exploding won't work with me."

Use body language to end the insult. Look bored, yawn and wave the person away.

Summary:

1. *Use "I messages."*
2. *Use small talk.*
3. *Invite kids to talk about feelings.*
4. *Try the Sweet and Sour Approach.*
5. *Always provide face-saving comments.*
6. *Use silence.*
7. *Match your words to your body language.*
8. *Invite an angry student to sit.*

Dear Carol,

Your book arrived the Friday before the first day of school. I was able to read it and implement your strategies from day one.

This was the first year I didn't give my students the long list of do's and don'ts. What a relief! I always knew they mostly tune that out. Instead, I used the Student Information Sheet. I've enjoyed reading about their summer experiences.

The other thing they liked was hearing about me. I'm almost embarrassed to tell you that in 12 years of teaching I have never shared much personal information about myself.

I've implemented the homework log, the make-up file, the class rules and beginning class with culture questions on the overhead. This buys me time to take roll, collect money, etc.

I love all your tips and feel I have command over my day! Thank you for writing a helpful, practical book. I'm passing it onto my colleagues.

Sincerely,
Lynn Chiodo, High school, French teacher
Merritt Island, Florida

Please Share With Us

We receive emails, notes and letters from teachers and administrators sharing strategies, techniques and good ideas for running a classroom. Professional educators share what they know.

You might wish to share any new method you've used and loved. These might include: letters home, assignments, school and classroom pictures, personal stories, reading strategies, classrooms rules and procedures, etc.

Send to:
Carol Fuery
P.O. Box 461
Captiva FL 33924
teach@carolfuery.com
www.carolfuery.com
fax: 239-472-0699

Afterword

We learn by doing. Your first year will be your hardest. We learn from our mistakes and hopefully through the use of this book, your mistakes will be small ones. As you teach, refer to this manual. Make notes in it. You're changing more than you know. You're learning a profession, so be patient with yourself and your students. And remember every teacher was once a new teacher.

The next few years will be turbulent, terrifying and adventuresome. Learn from your setbacks as well as your successes. Remember that a ship in port is safe, but that's not what ships were built for.

Be brave. You have nothing to lose and everything to gain. You're embarking on a safari to uncover your authentic self. It takes courage to be who you are. You're powerful, talented and trained. Enter your school, open your classroom door, and know that you need not take it or leave it as it was when you came in.

Carol Fuery

SOME HELPFUL WEBSITES

Organizations

Association of Teacher Educators
www.edweek.org/context/orgs/ate.htm
A national membership organization.

Education Week on the Web
www.edweek.org
Education news: Keep up with what's new!

Educational Resources Information Center (ERIC)
www.accesseric.org/home.html
Find all significant documents related to education.

National Center for Education Statistics
www.nces.ed.gov
The primary agency responsible for collecting and analyzing data related to education in the U.S. and other countries.

National Council Teachers of English
www.ncte.org
Professional organization for literacy and language arts.

National PTA
www.pta.org
The website for the national parent-teacher volunteer organization. Bulletin boards and lists of events.

Dr. Andrew Weil's Self Healing
www.dr.weilselfhealing.com
Health for mind and body, free newsletter.

U.S. Department of Education
www.ed.gov
The government agency that oversees education provides information and research.

Word Games and Art
www.edgamesandart.com/ptalinks.html
Links to parent-teacher associations; organizations for parents, teachers, and early childhood educators.

Resources

Academic Software
www.academicsoftwareusa.com
Academic software at competitive prices.

Arizona State Public Information Network: Teacher Resources
http://aspin.asu.edu/-casey/webresources/
Lesson plans, curricula and classroom ideas.

AskERIC
http://ericir.syr.edu
Resources compiled in response to teachers' questions to the Educational Resources Information Center.

Ball Elementary (IL): Teacher Resources
http://bes.bcsd.k12.il.us/teach.htm
Ideas, lesson plans, resources on any topic.

The BIG PAGES of Teacher Resource Sites
www.mts.net/-jgreenco/teacher.html
Recommends general teaching sites

Birch Lane School (CA): Teacher Resources
http://birchlane,davis.ca.us/webstuff/teach.htm
Online lessons, activities, projects, resources and references for teachers.

Continental Press
www.continentalpress.com
Publisher of supplemental education materials.

Creative Publications
www.creativepublications.com
Publisher of supplemental products for math education.

Dorseyville Middle School (PA): Links for Music Teachers
www.fcasd.edu/schools/dms/tmu.htm
Important links for music education.

Educational Insights
www.educationalinsights.com
Educational toys and games.

EdWeb
http://edweb.gsn.org
Information for educators regarding technology and school reform.

Encarta Schoolhouse
www.encarta.msn.com/Schoolhouse
Resources for educators in grades 7-12, featuring Microsoft facts and links.

The Explorer
http://explorer.scrtec.org
Math and science resources for grades K-12.

Free Lesson Plans
www.lessonplanspage.com
Provides curriculum materials.

Glenbrook North (IL) Mathematics Department Teacher Resources
www.glenbrook.k12.il.us/gbnmath/TR.htm.
Resources and lesson plans for Math.

Internet Resources for Teacher Librarians: Teacher Development
www3.sympatico.ca/rbudding/tlresources/tchrdevt.htm
Materials, lesson plans and classroom activities.

Lakeshore Learning Materials
www.lakeshorelearning.com
Materials for early childhood education and grades 1-3.

Los Angeles County Office of Education: Conferences and Events
http://teams.lacoe.edu/documentation/news/conferences.html
Information on educational conferences.

Meridian Joint School District (ID): Links for Teachers
www.sd02.k12.id.us/103/Iteach.htm
Resources, curriculum ideas, and guides to other internet sites.

myteacher.net: Teacher Links
http://myteacher.net/edresources/teacher.html
Links for resources, products, and organizations.

The National Science Foundation
www.nsf.gov
The independent U.S. government agency that promotes science and engineering through research and education projects.

Northern Lebanon (PA) School District: Web Links for Students and Teachers
www.norleb.k12.pa.us/documents/links.htm
Links for math, science, social studies, language arts and other topics.

PE Central
http://pe.central.vt.edu
Information for health and physical education teachers.

Perfection Learning
www.perfectionlearning.com
Publisher of curriculum materials for grades K-12.

Sanibel SandDollar Publishing
www.carolfuery.com
Activities for K-12, teaching strategies, motivational ideas, classroom management books and seminars.

Scholastic Professional Books
http://teacher.scholastic.com/index.htm
Lesson plans, reproducibles, authors and books, online activities, research tools, book and software clubs, and reading programs.

Teaching Resource Center
www.trcabc.com/teaching_resource_materials/sch_supls.htm
Resource materials and supplies at competitive prices.

Teaching Tolerance
www.teachingtolerance.org
A website dedicated to unbiased education practices. News, articles, teaching ideas, resources, and literature.

Teachers.Net
www.teachers.net
Teacher resources, reference tools, and forums.

Teacher Support Software
www.tssoftware.com
Publisher of educational software.

United Art and Education Supply Co.
www.unitednow.com
School supplies and materials.

Support Groups

Links2Go: K12 Newsgroups
www.links2go.com/more/www.liszt.com/news/k12
Teacher newsgroups; links to topics related to K-12 teaching.

SchoolNotes.com
www.schoolnotes.com
Educators can post notes and homework for their students.

Teacher Talk Home Page
http://education.indiana.edu/cas/tt/tthmpg.htm.
Website for pre-service and secondary-education teachers, sponsored by the Indiana University School of Education.

Teacher.Net
www.teachers.net
Information for teachers, opportunities to ask questions.

Violence Prevention

Early Warning, Timely Response:
A Guide to Safe Schools
www.ed.gov/offices/OSERS/OSEP/earlywrn.html
A violence prevention guide based on the work of an independent panel of experts in the fields of education, law enforcement and mental health.

Keep Schools Safe
www.keepschoolssafe.org
Resources to help make schools safer and help prevent violence.

National Crime Prevention Council:
Stopping School Violence
www.ncpc.org/2schvio.htm
Prevention information, links to resources.

National Criminal Justice Reference Service
http://www.ncjrs.org/works
Preventing crime: what works, what doesn't and what's promising.

National Resource Center for Safe Schools:
The Safety Zone
www.safetyzone.org
The National Resource Center for Safe Schools works to create safe learning environments.

The Network of Violence Prevention Practitioners
www2.edc.org/nvpp
A global forum for exchanging information, opportunities for professional development, and dialogue between practitioners, researchers, evaluators, and policy makers to improve violence prevention.

Partnerships Against Violence Network
www.pavnet.org
Information about violence and youth-at-risk.

Security is mostly a superstition. It does not exist in nature, nor do the children of men as a whole experience. Avoiding danger is no safer in the long run than outright exposure. Life is either a daring adventure or nothing.

-Helen Keller

Index

www.carolfuery.com
Where teachers and administrators go for answers

Quick Order Form

Fax orders: 239-472-0699 Send this Form

Telephone orders: Call 800-330-3459 toll free. Have your credit card ready.

Email orders: teach@carolfuery.com

Mail orders: Sanibel SandDollar Publishing, P.O. Box 461, Captiva, FL 33924 USA
Telephone: 239-472-3459

Please send more FREE information on:

☐ Other Books   ☐ Speaking/Seminars   ☐ Consulting

Billing/Shipping Information:

Name, Title: _____

Organization: _____

Address: _____

City, State, Zip, County: _____

E-Mail: _____

Phone: _____ Fax: _____

Method of Payment:

☐ Check payable to Sanibel SandDollar Publications   ☐ **VISA**   ☐ **MasterCard**

Card #: _____ Expiration Date: _____

Name on Card: _____

Signature: _____

Please send the following books:

TITLE	QTY.	PRICE	TOTAL
Winning Year One	_____	$15.95	_____
Still Teaching After All These Years	_____	$15.95	_____
Discipline Strategies (Classroom Management)	_____	$15.95	_____
Successful Subbing	_____	$11.95	_____

Sales tax: Add 6% for Florida individuals (not schools or districts).
Domestic Shipping/Handling: $5.00 for first book, $2.00 each additional.
International: Call for rates. Discounts on bulk orders. Orders over $100 add 8%
shipping; AK, HI, Canada add 18%.
Quantity Discounts Available.

Subtotal _____

FL Res. 6% Sales Tax _____

Shipping _____

Total Due _____

www.carolfuery.com
Where teachers and administrators go for answers

Quick Order Form

Fax orders: 239-472-0699 Send this Form

Telephone orders: Call 800-330-3459 toll free. Have your credit card ready.

Email orders: teach@carolfuery.com

Mail orders: Sanibel SandDollar Publishing, P.O. Box 461, Captiva, FL 33924 USA
Telephone: 239-472-3459

Please send more FREE information on:

☐ Other Books   ☐ Speaking/Seminars   ☐ Consulting

Billing/Shipping Information:

Name, Title: _____

Organization: _____

Address: _____

City, State, Zip, County: _____

E-Mail: _____

Phone: _____ Fax: _____

Method of Payment:

☐ Check payable to Sanibel SandDollar Publications   ☐ **VISA**   ☐ **MasterCard**

Card #: _____ Expiration Date: _____

Name on Card: _____

Signature: _____

Please send the following books:

TITLE	QTY.	PRICE	TOTAL
Winning Year One	_____	$15.95	_____
Still Teaching After All These Years	_____	$15.95	_____
Discipline Strategies (Classroom Management)	_____	$15.95	_____
Successful Subbing	_____	$11.95	_____

Sales tax: Add 6% for Florida individuals (not schools or districts).
Domestic Shipping/Handling: $5.00 for first book, $2.00 each additional.
International: Call for rates. Discounts on bulk orders. Orders over $100 add 8%
shipping; AK, HI, Canada add 18%.
Quantity Discounts Available.

Subtotal _____

FL Res. 6% Sales Tax _____

Shipping _____

Total Due _____

www.carolfuery.com
Where teachers and administrators go for answers

Quick Order Form

Fax orders: 239-472-0699 Send this Form

Telephone orders: Call 800-330-3459 toll free. Have your credit card ready.

Email orders: teach@carolfuery.com

Mail orders: Sanibel SandDollar Publishing, P.O. Box 461, Captiva, FL 33924 USA
Telephone: 239-472-3459

Please send more FREE information on:

☐ Other Books   ☐ Speaking/Seminars   ☐ Consulting

Billing/Shipping Information:

Name, Title: _____

Organization: _____

Address: _____

City, State, Zip, County: _____

E-Mail: _____

Phone: _____ Fax: _____

Method of Payment:

☐ Check payable to Sanibel SandDollar Publications   ☐ **VISA**   ☐ **MasterCard**

Card #: _____ Expiration Date: _____

Name on Card: _____

Signature: _____

Please send the following books:

TITLE	QTY.	PRICE	TOTAL
Winning Year One	_____	$15.95	_____
Still Teaching After All These Years	_____	$15.95	_____
Discipline Strategies (Classroom Management)	_____	$15.95	_____
Successful Subbing	_____	$11.95	_____

Sales tax: Add 6% for Florida individuals (not schools or districts).
Domestic Shipping/Handling: $5.00 for first book, $2.00 each additional.
International: Call for rates. Discounts on bulk orders. Orders over $100 add 8%
shipping; AK, HI, Canada add 18%.
Quantity Discounts Available.

Subtotal _____

FL Res. 6% Sales Tax _____

Shipping _____

Total Due _____